The Entrepreneur's Blueprint

How to stop working and make a fortune

– even in your sleep!

by

Russell Leeds

LEGAL NOTICES

The information presented herein represents the view of the authors as of the date of publication. Because of the rate with which conditions change, the author reserves the right to alter and update his opinion based on the new conditions. This book is for informational purposes only. While every attempt has been made to verify the information provided in this book, neither the authors nor their affiliates/partners assume any responsibility for errors, inaccuracies or omissions. Any slights of people or organisations are unintentional. You should be aware of any laws which govern business transactions or other business practices in your country and state. Any reference to any person or business whether living or dead is purely coincidental.

Every effort has been made to accurately represent this product and its potential. Examples in these materials are not to be interpreted as a promise or guarantee of earnings. Earning potential is entirely dependent on the person using our product, ideas and techniques. We do not purport this as a "get rich scheme."

Your level of success in attaining the results claimed in our materials depends on the time you devote to the program, ideas and techniques mentioned your finances, knowledge and various skills. Since these factors differ according to individuals, we cannot guarantee your success or income level. Nor are we responsible for any of your actions.

Any and all forward looking statements here or on any of our sales material are intended to express our opinion of earnings potential. Many factors will be important in determining your actual results and no guarantees are made that you will achieve results similar to ours or anybody else's, in fact no guarantees are made that you will achieve any results from our ideas and techniques in our material.

The Entrepreneur's Blueprint

How to stop working and make a fortune

– even in your sleep!

by

Russell Leeds

CONTENTS

Foreword

So why did I decide to write this book? I wanted to share with you the exact steps anyone can take and apply to any business which will allow you to retire in three years or less –

on a handsome wage of £100,000 per year, I might add.

This will not only be great for you, but also for your friends, family, children and the country as a whole. Entrepreneurship sparks economic growth. We need more successful entrepreneurs to help grow our economy. If you, as an entrepreneur, are successful it will benefit everyone.

Sadly 80 per cent of new businesses collapse within the first five years. Meaning only 20 per cent survive, perhaps even scarier, 80 per cent of those businesses fail in the next five years.

I believe the primary reason is a lack of education. Schools do not teach children how to become entrepreneurs, nor how to start and run a business. Our whole society is geared towards getting a job.

I wrote this book to help equip business owners with all the knowledge and expertise I have gathered through years of experience running my own businesses, as well as from books, seminars, courses, business coaches and mentors.

By reading this book you will learn *The Entrepreneur's Blueprint* – the precise steps you need to take to choose the right business, systemise and replicate it, dominate your market and be more successful than right now you probably believe is possible.

If you follow the system and so desire, you too can stop working and still be making thousands of pounds in profit every single month.

Chapter 1 - Who Am I To Tell You?

Six years ago, I was running my own entertainment company. I did all the work and was making a profit of about £20,000 a year. Fast forward to today and I own several successful companies that make hundreds of thousands of pounds every month. I also have a fantastic team of staff doing most of the work.

So, what changed to create this sudden transformation?
I had always worked hard but didn't really know what I was doing. To be honest I was winging it.

The truth is it does not matter who you are, or how good you are. You will never be able to figure out everything yourself. Even the best and most successful entrepreneurs still have advisers, mentors and coaches. They still continue to study, learn and improve themselves.

This was something I had never really done. I felt that once I left school, my education was over and it was time to work. How wrong was I? The crazy thing is, the more successful I have become, the more time I spend educating myself. Listening to audio books while I am driving is one of my favourite ways to learn as it feels like a really good use of time. I also read books, I have a business coach and I spend thousands of pounds on seminars and training events. Never be too proud to learn. The fact you are reading this book shows me that you too have a desire to learn and educate yourself.

This book is aimed at people who already have a small business or want to start their own business with a burning desire to see it explode over the next few years.

I will take you through the steps and systems I used to dramatically change my life and catapult my businesses to more success than I ever dreamed was possible.

So, as you're going to be spending some time reading what I have to say, I thought I would start by telling you about myself.

My story

I was born into a lower middle-class family, just outside Wolverhampton, in February 1989.

I have two younger siblings – a brother, Samuel, who is just two years younger than me, and a sister, Tiffany, who is six years younger. I have always got on well with them and still do to this day. We did everything together when we were younger.

When I was eight years old my parents sent us all to a tiny Christian school in Walsall. It was a heck of a commute as we lived 13 miles away. With the usual rush hour traffic, it could take us over an hour to get there.

There were only 60 pupils in the whole school, but it was great, and I only have fond memories of my time there. I also made some good friends who I am still in touch with. More importantly, I met my first girlfriend. Her name was Anna and we have just celebrated our eleventh wedding anniversary.

My childhood was mostly terrific, although my parents did go through a messy divorce when I was nine. They both remarried, but I guess there were also some tough times.

I do not know whether you can relate to this, but sometimes other people have a plan for your life, and it is just expected that you will do it.

That is exactly what happened to me. My father was a magician/entertainer and he expected Samuel and I to follow in his footsteps. Most parents want their children to go into further education such as A-levels or university.

This was not the path laid out for me. I was to leave school at 16, then go to work for my dad, and his business partner Craig, as a children's entertainer.

It was just a small company. I was the only employee, but they were doing reasonably well getting work and keeping busy. It was probably the last job I wanted to do as I was always quite shy as a child. Getting up in front of a large group of children and adults to perform magic, scared the living daylights out of me.

My job was to attend children's parties and to run, host and do everything for the parents so they could relax and enjoy the occasion. I did this through a mixture of party games, balloon modelling and a comedy magic show.

Three days before my first gig I was already feeling physically sick as I was so nervous. It was just a one-hour party in Wolverhampton, but I can still vividly remember knocking on the front door and hoping the parents would not answer.

They did of course. I cannot remember much about the party itself as I have a tendency to forget bad memories, but it was a real struggle.

It was an incredibly tough ask for a shy 16-year-old who had little training and no work experience. I persevered, however, and a couple of years later I was fantastic at my job. I was also getting great feedback from all the clients and earning a reasonable salary.

At the same time, I was studying close-up magic. This is the sort of magic you may have seen Dynamo or David Blaine perform on television – small tricks with cards, coins, string and rubber bands.

The year 2008 was great for me because, after dating for five years, Anna and I tied the knot. We were both young, but I knew she was the one. It was an absolutely amazing day and we moved into our first home the next day. It was a new build, two-bedroom apartment in Walsall.

Now aged 19 I was a pretty good close-up magician. I had just released my first magic DVD called *Banding Around* through a well-known company and it was a massive success amongst magicians.

I then got selected to compete in the Close Up Magician of the Year European Championships. At the time I was the youngest person ever to compete. I did not win but it was a great experience, and I felt massively honoured just to be taking part.

In 2011, my dad, Craig and I set up a new entertainment company called *Slightly Unusual* which provided a large, grand illusion show with saw-a-lady-in-half type tricks. The act consisted of myself, Craig and my wife Anna as 'the glamorous assistant.'

We spent about a year putting the show together and trying to get it as good as it could possibly be. Our unique selling point was that it was a comedy illusion show in which we did not take ourselves too seriously.

Craig played the arrogant, bumbling buffoon. I was the skilled straight guy, while Anna portrayed a moody assistant who was aware of how useless we really were.

This was great for me because for the first time I wasn't just an employee, but actually got the chance to get involved in the business side.

We targeted weddings and corporate events and realised that we could charge about five times as much for illusion shows than children's parties.

I really enjoyed all the business planning and coming up with new ways to make more money. Craig, Anna and I would spend hours poring over business books and listening to audio tapes on our long van journeys. We were learning so much and *Slightly Unusual* was becoming successful.

One of our main strategies was to create lots of 'social proof'. We worked really hard at writing press releases, performing at fringe festivals and charity events for free, contacting television companies, creating our own YouTube show – anything we could think of to get our name and face out there. As a result, in a few breath-taking years we could boast that we had:

- Won Brit Idol 2012
- Reached the finals of Britain Does Variety 2012
- Performed on ITV1, Sky and German television

We were also officially named the Most Loved Entertainers in the UK for two consecutive years in 2012 and 2013.

I enjoyed success in my own right too after winning the coveted titles of British Magical Society Close Up Magician of the Year and the British Magical Society Stage Magician of the Year.

Rave reviews for our show started rolling in from some of the country's leading personalities and respected media.

'Really Funny' – Sir Ken Dodd

'Totally Amazing' – Alan Titchmarsh

'Imagine if Morecambe and Wise performed the illusions of David Copperfield' – HRC Radio

'The speciality act of the decade' – The Stage Newspaper

'The most groundbreaking, original and fresh act in years' – The Stage Newspaper

Having all this 'social proof' allowed us to position ourselves as the absolute best in our field. That meant we could charge more and do more prestigious shows.

On the outside it was all rosy, but I did not particularly enjoy working with my father, especially now that I was his business partner in *Slightly Unusual*.

I realised that in truth it was never going to be a partnership and he was always going to see me as an employee.

I had big ideas and plans, and knew I needed to leave to do my own thing.

It was awkward because I did not want to set myself up in competition with him, so I decided to leave the world of magic and establish my own business, managing property.

I handed in my notice in 2013. Soon afterwards, my father and Craig decided to go their separate ways, with my father actually moving to Brazil.

Craig contacted me and asked if I would be interested in buying out my father's share in *Slightly Unusual*.

Craig and I had worked very well together. We both had different strengths and weaknesses. So, after speaking to my father and getting his blessing, I put the property business on hold and re-joined Craig.

Slightly Unusual went from strength to strength and we were turning over more money than we could ever have imagined.

In June 2014, Anna and I had our first child, a girl. We named her Sienna and the next year Anna gave birth to our second daughter, Emily. These were without doubt the best days of my life. Having children is the biggest blessing. It can be extremely hard work with the sleepless nights and changing nappies, but it is amazing.

Although we were doing very well and it was a lot of fun, we were now parents.
Going away on lengthy tours and getting home at 4am was no longer particularly desirable.

This was when I truly realised the difference between active and passive income.

Active income is what most people have. It does not matter if you run your own business, or have a job, you will most likely receive an active income.

It works like this: you do some work, whatever it might be, and then you get paid for it. If you stopped working, you would stop getting paid.

Passive income comes from doing some work and then continuing to get paid for it, every single day. If you are sunbathing in the Bahamas, spending time with your children, or doing whatever you desire, you still get paid. However, creating a passive income is something that most business owners do not do. They themselves are essential to the day-to-day running of the company.

In this book you will learn how to turn your enterprise into passive income so that you only work when you want to, not because you have to.

So back to my story. In 2013, we set up a second business called Non Stop Kids Entertainment. It was a children's entertainment company, so I had quite a lot of experience in the field. However, the big difference was that I was not going to be the entertainer. This would be someone else and I would be taking a cut - that was the start of generating a passive income for myself.

Every year, from 2013 to 2017, Non Stop Kids doubled in size. By 2017, we had more than 30 full-time entertainers and a team in the office dealing with all the marketing, sales and general administration. It was a passive income as I no longer had to get involved at all.

To put things in perspective, in 2013, I was living in a small, two-bedroom council house and driving a 10-year-old Skoda. Three years later, I had moved into a seven-bedroom, 17th century cottage in a small village just outside Lichfield and was driving a new Mercedes GLE, as well as a Porsche.

So given I now had more time on my hands with passive income, I went back to thinking about property and decided in 2017 to buy a struggling lettings agency. I rebranded it and, using the *Entrepreneur's Blueprint* that had been so successful with Non Stop Kids Entertainment, dramatically turned it around.

At around the same time, my brother Samuel was doing very well as a businessman himself. We had a healthy rivalry where we would compare who was earning more, turning over more, had nicer offices, better staff... Although we were both highly competitive, we also would help and advise each other a great deal. We both secretly admired what each other was doing. I was particularly impressed with his property training, the number of people attending his courses and the incredibly high success rate of his students. So many of them were getting life-changing results; it really was incredible to witness.

In 2018, Samuel asked whether I'd consider merging our companies and working together. This was something new and exciting. I didn't take much persuading. I sold the entertainment companies to Craig as they didn't fit with our new vision moving forward.

My two primary businesses are now property investment/development and training people to be successful as an entrepreneur and investor. For more details check out www.russell-leeds.com.

Since implementing the systems described in this book into our new businesses, we are on track to make a profit of about £7m this year.

I truly believe that with the right knowledge and work ethic, anyone in our country has the resources available to be extremely happy and successful.

With that in mind, I'm sure you are ready to learn the *Entrepreneur's Blueprint* and become a millionaire, have plenty of spare time, travel the world or do whatever it is you desire in the next three years.

Chapter 2 – Five Steps To Choosing The R.I.G.H.T. Business

Sometimes you hear of people who have become an overnight success. This is rarely the case. There will have always been some smart, hard work that has gone unnoticed in the background.

Lionel Messi, one of the best (if not THE best) footballers to ever grace the planet, said: 'It took me 17 years and 114 days to become an overnight success.'

People say he became an instant success, but they did not see the years of hard work, toil, and discipline he endured. As a youngster he was often terribly homesick. To become the best player in the world Messi also had to overcome various illnesses and family issues.

The *Entrepreneur's Blueprint* will allow you to become successful in a short space of time, but it will not be overnight.

One of the most important and certainly the first question you should ask yourself is, what is my business going to be? It is key to get this right, otherwise you might be working really hard at a business that is never going to succeed.

Now it might be that you already have a business and you're thinking: "Oh I can skip this chapter because I already know what I want to do." I strongly urge you to reconsider. Make sure your current business ticks the following five boxes. If it doesn't, what is the point of carrying on with it? You will never be successful. Sure, you might have limited success, but why limit yourself? Why work harder than you need to?

Most people set up a business because it is something they can do or something they expect they will enjoy doing.

So they think to themselves: "I like the idea of being an accountant. I'll train to be an accountant and set up my own business." They then run that business as a sole trader and as a result they do absolutely everything in that business. So, as well as the actual accountancy, they will also do the bookkeeping, marketing and business planning, they'll be making the sales calls, they'll be providing the customer service, they'll man the reception and so on.

Now this is fine if you want to create a job where you can earn decent money and be your own boss – and when setting up your first business, you will almost certainly have to do that in the early stages.

However, if you're only getting paid when you do the work, it means you're limiting the amount of money you can earn. Even if you were being paid £100 per hour, and working 40 hours weeks, you would still only be turning over a maximum of £200,000 per year. You would also be working way too hard because you wouldn't be getting paid for all the other activities that need to be done in every business, such as the marketing, book-keeping planning, and so on.

Warren Buffet, one of the richest and most successful businessmen in the world, says this:

> *"If you don't find a way to make money while you sleep, you will work until you die."*

What you need to do is have a business that you can replicate, a business that can make a profit while other people do the work for you, a business that makes money even when you're asleep.

People say to me: "But Russell, I don't want the hassle of having staff."

> "Fine," I say. "Don't, but you will never be successful. So get over yourself and realise that you can't make it on your own. You need other people. Name one successful business that has no staff. No, I didn't think you could."

Luckily, pretty much every business going can have employees and can be replicated. I even managed to make it work as a children's entertainer.

So I'm now going to take you through my *Five-Step Guide to Choosing the Right Business.* I use this guide before buying, investing or developing any new business, and you should too, to ensure you're putting your valuable time into the right business.

Before I reveal my Five-Step Guide, here's a neat segue into those five steps:

There's a very interesting and popular entrepreneurial TV show in the UK called Dragons Den, where budding entrepreneurs get three minutes to pitch their business ideas to five multimillionaires who are willing to invest their own cash to kick-start businesses. After each pitch, the Dragons have the opportunity to ask questions about the venture. The entrepreneurs don't have to answer, but of course what they choose to say will affect the Dragons' decision to invest (or not). The pitch is over and declared unsuccessful when each Dragon has declared, "I'm out."

Quite often the entrepreneur has spent years and hundreds of thousands of pounds investing in their idea, only to be told by an experienced Dragon to stop wasting their time, as it's not a good business idea and will never work.

Do not let that be you. If the budding entrepreneur had put their business idea through the 5-step "**R.I.G.H.T**". Guide, they could have saved an awful lot of time and money.

R is for "Replicate"

Can you replicate your business?

If you want to grow a £1m business, it is essential that you don't have to be hands on. This will give you the time to plan and grow the business.

At the start, you will most likely need to do everything yourself. However, as soon as you can afford to, take on employees or independent contractors to do as many of the tasks as possible for you.

My goal when I set up a business is not to be needed at all. The business must be able to function without me. This can be hard, especially if you like to control every situation.

I'll give you an example of how much more money you can make if you have a business model that you can replicate, as follows:

> Most children's entertainers can deliver about four parties over a weekend, so if I just did parties myself, based on the figures above, I would make £180 x 4 = £720 per weekend.
>
> However, if I gave the parties to one of our entertainers, I would make £77 x 4 = £308. The table below sets out how much I would earn with a different number of entertainers:

2 entertainers £77 x 4 x 2 = £616
4 entertainers £77 x 4 x 4 = £1,232
20 entertainers £77 x 4 x 20 = £6,160
50 entertainers £77 x 4 x 50 = £15,400
100 entertainers £77 x 4 x 100 = £30,800

There is clearly no way that I could make £30,800 profit over a weekend (£1.6m a year) delivering kids' parties if I were doing all the work myself.

In most small businesses, the owner is the business. Do not let this be you. If you let this happen and you become successful, you will soon burn out because you'll be doing all the work to keep up with demand.

There are three roles in any business: the workers, the managers and the entrepreneur.

As the business owner, your job is to be the entrepreneur. Your role is to plan how it can grow and come up with innovative ideas which can make that happen.

If you spend your time working in and managing the business, you will not have the time to grow it.

If your sales increased tomorrow by 500 percent, could you cope? Do you have the systems in place to allow that to happen? If not, that is what you need to spend your time doing.

Make sure you have brilliant systems that your staff can easily understand. This also means that when a member of staff leaves, it won't cause a problem because the systems are easy to understand for new staff.

I would also highly recommend writing a training manual that covers everything your workforce has to do. As well as making it easier for new employees, it also ensures that everyone who works at your company delivers the same level of service. Do not underestimate the importance of delivering the same experience to your customer when they re-use you.

Consistency Is King.

It would be better to be consistently average than amazing the first time, good on the second occasion and below average the third time.

People like to use companies when they know what they're going to get. For example, I like eating my lunch at Subway because the food is remarkably consistent. No matter where in the country I go, I know exactly what I'm going to get.

I is for "In demand"

Is your product or service in demand?

You'll have to do your research and look at other companies that already do what you plan to do. How much do they make? How busy are they?

You might think: "Hey, nobody's doing what I want to do, so there's a gap in the market." If nobody's doing it, chances are there's no demand for it.

It is usually best if there are already companies doing the same thing that are successful, so that you know the business model works and can then try to emulate them. This way you're not going to spend years trying to sell something that people just don't want.

There are exceptions to that rule, but they are few and far between. Even Uber, which is totally unique in the way it provides its service, is in many ways a taxi company and is still targeting the same market as all the other taxi firms. Uber is just doing it in a more innovative and cost-effective way.

G is for Good profit margin?

Is there a good profit margin?
This is really important because if you're not making a good profit, then what's the point of doing it?

You need a good understanding of the industry and the costs involved in running the business. How much will you need to spend on advertising? How much will it cost to get someone else to do the job for you?

As an example, let's take a look at the set-up I had with my children's entertainment agency:

> I charged the customer £180 for an entertainer to run a party for two hours. The price I paid the entertainer (this is the person who will go to the party and keep the children and adults entertained) was £84.
>
> We spent £10 on marketing. We actually spent thousands of pounds every month on advertising but we tracked everything. It usually worked out at about the £10 mark for every gig.
>
> A further £9 went on sales and administration. We had office staff who answered the phone, took and processed the bookings and it worked out at roughly £9 per party.
>
> This left a profit of £77 per party which was a profit margin of 42.8 percent. For the service industry that is pretty good.

Of course, there will be other monthly costs associated with running a business, such as office rent, CRM systems, telephone call packages, bookkeeping, HR support and insurance. However, these costs tend to stay the same, so if you manage to grow the business and take more bookings, your profit will inevitably increase.

You should work out your profit margin by assuming that you're not going to be doing any of the work. In this way, you'll be able to see whether the business will remain profitable as it grows.

You either need to be making good profits from your sales or be selling in such vast bulk that you're still making healthy margins. I think it's easier to focus on making a good profit from every sale.

H is for "High Barrier"

A friend of mine, called Hayley, is a mobile hairdresser. She's very experienced and very good and she runs her own business. She makes decent money, around £25 per hour, and she loves the flexibility of managing her own diary as it allows her to manage her social life, the school run and gives her the flexibility she needs.

Mobile hairdressing is a very easy business to start, assuming you can cut hair, I certainly wouldn't be able to do it.

Start up costs are very low, all you need to buy is a bag, scissors, hair clippers, a few other products and you're pretty much good to go.

Hayley had worked out that hairdressers who worked in salons in the local area only got paid £8.50 per hour, which was approximately a third of what she was getting as a mobile hairdresser, and she suddenly had a great idea. She could employ hairdressers to do her round and build a team. She could replicate her business and be earning far more than she was earning now.

Hayley planned to pay her team £12 an hour, far more than they could earn at a salon. She'd only need 2 employees, she wouldn't need to cut anyone's hair again and she'd be making just as much money as she was earning now.

Unfortunately, Hayley's plan didn't work. She was unable to keep her staff happy, they would all leave and very quickly.

But why? Was it because Hayley was a horrible boss? No, it was simply because it wasn't a high barrier to entry business. The new hairdressers realised they could just get their own clients and earn 100% of the money themselves.

High barrier to entry is your friend and you certainly don't want a low barrier to entry business.

Adopting this mantra will be invaluable in making sure you have the right business to scale up so that you can be turning over £1m plus.

So what is a high barrier to entry?

High barrier to entry means there are barriers in your way that will make it difficult for you to start your business.

Typical barriers would be:

- A large investment required
- Difficult qualifications to achieve
- Expensive equipment or buildings to acquire
- Regulations to comply with

Now you might think: "Surely having fewer barriers in the way would make it better and easier."

The problem is if it is easy for you, it is easy for everyone.

So, even if you stumble across a great idea, everyone could be doing it and soon will be doing it. Worse still, when you try to scale up your business, your staff will leave and try to do it themselves, which is exactly what happened to Hayley.

This means that if there are lots of obstacles and red tape in the way, making it difficult to start your enterprise, you should be delighted and say: "I'm prepared to go through all the hassle that 99 percent of people wouldn't bother with, so in the long run it will be easier to scale up my business and be successful."

T is for "True"

Are you being true to yourself? Are you really passionate about it?

Many budding entrepreneurs will start a new business because they think it's a great way to make money. However, if you don't have a passion for what you do, then don't do it. If you're not being true to yourself, you won't stick to it when the going gets tough. Money is one motivating factor, but even stronger than money is a mission. If you can combine money and mission that is when you're going to become truly unstoppable.

Steve Jobs put it like this:

> "*You have to have a lot of passion for what you are doing because it is so hard… if you don't, any rational person would give up.*"

If you're passionate about your business, you'll love what you do, you'll work harder, practise harder and become unbeatable.

If you're passionate about your business and what you're trying to achieve, you're much more likely to succeed. You'll be able to attract high-calibre team members, clients and investors because they'll feed off your enthusiasm. When you speak, people will buy into what you're saying because they'll feel your passion, they'll sense that you're being true to yourself.

As you know, I became an entertainer and more specifically a magician as soon as I left school, aged 16. My first ever gig was at a children's birthday party being held at a rather nice village hall on the outskirts of Wolverhampton.

Being just 16, I was unable to drive but I arranged a lift from my stepfather Tim. He dropped me off at the front of the venue and I can vividly remember the back of his black Ford Focus slowly disappearing out of sight as he drove away.

I was incredibly nervous as I was expected to keep Molly, who was celebrating her fifth birthday, and her 30 friends entertained for a full two hours. At this point I had only been performing 'professionally' (and I use that word loosely) for about two weeks.

On entering the room, I started walking around aimlessly asking for Sarah, Molly's mum.

I eventually found her, introduced myself and slowly started setting up my equipment. I didn't have much with me – a small silver case which contained a handful of second-hand magic tricks, a balloon pump and a bag of Qualatex modelling balloons. I also had a green sports bag full of bits and pieces which I had put together for party games.

Looking back, I was highly inexperienced, had virtually no training, did not have all the necessary equipment and did not have the confidence to pull it off.

To be honest, I can't remember much about the actual party. As I said, I tend to block out bad memories and focus on the good ones. Maybe it's because I'm an optimist.

But what I do remember is that about halfway through the party, Sarah came storming over.

She said: "Can I have a word?"

"Yes, of course," I replied, following her out into the cold hallway.

"I'm going to be honest with you," said Sarah.

> "Last year we hired Jimbo. He was great. The year before we hired Dizzy Lizzy who was also very good."

(Jimbo and Dizzy Lizzy were well established entertainers in my area when I first started).

> "This year I wanted to hire the best and came across your website, so I hired you. I've never been so disappointed in my entire life. You've lost control of the children. I think I'd be better off finishing the party on my own."

Sarah handed me £70 in cash, which was just under half of the £150 fee, and said:

"I'm going to pay you for the work you've done, but please just leave.'

I went back in the room, quickly packed away my props and left. I called Tim and asked if he could come back earlier than planned as I had now finished.

It was dark outside and, as I sat on the side of the road, tears streamed down my cheeks. I felt humiliated and worthless, waiting for Tim to pick me up.

So why on earth, given how terrible I was, and how stressed it had made me feel, did I carry on trying to make it as an entertainer?

The answer was that I had a passion for magic, even though I had been pretty much forced into it. I was totally sold on magic. I loved performing it and I knew that if I carried on, I would get good at it. I knew that I would succeed.

Without that fire in my belly, I would have quit for sure.

Back in 2005, if you had told that shy 16-year-old that he would go on to win an award at the UK Children's Entertainer of the Year National Championships, perform magic live on TV and run one of the largest children's entertainment agencies in the UK – providing entertainment at thousands of events every year – he probably would not have believed you. None of those achievements would have been possible without passion.

Chapter 3 - What Do You Want?

You could fill a whole library with books dedicated to goal setting and I would highly recommend really researching this and getting it right.

Without the right goals, you will lose motivation when things start getting tough.

Make sure that your short-term goals are realistic. Otherwise, when you don't achieve them, you'll feel disappointed and deflated. Ensure, however, that they're still tough enough to stretch you. The key is finding the right balance.

Long-term goals, by contrast, do not have to be realistic. Aim for the moon.

You should celebrate all your little achievements, even if you haven't quite hit your goal yet.

Personal goals

Start off by setting your personal goals. Examples could be:

- Taking two months' holiday a year
- Driving a new Range Rover
- Taking weekends off to spend time with the kids
- Playing golf once a week

Make sure these goals are really important to you and that they're not just targets you're writing down for the sake of it – even if that means you only have two or three goals. Make a list and do it now. Write down any goals you want to achieve in the next three years.

Three-year goals

1.

2.

3.

4.

5.

6.

7.

8.

After you've finished that, make a list of any goals that you'd like to achieve in the next year. These should be working towards attaining your three-year objectives.

One-year goals

1.

2.

3.

4.

5.

6.

7.

8.

Once you have your goals these will create your WHY?

Why are you working so hard?
Why are you never going to quit?
Why are you unstoppable?

Only once you have done this exercise, can you set your business goals, because they will facilitate your personal goals.

Most, if not all, your personal goals will come down to two factors: money and time.

To achieve your personal targets, you will need to be earning x amount of money and you will require x amount of time. Take time to work this out.

The great news is you now know exactly how much you want to be earning and how many days off you need over the year.

Targets

In three years' time I will be earning ________________ per year.

I will have ____________ weeks' annual leave.

I will take ____________ days off a week.

I have included the latter because, if you are anything like me, you will be tempted to work seven days a week. Make sure you don't.

The Parable of the Mexican Fisherman and the Banker

An American investment banker was taking a much-needed vacation in a Mexican coastal village when a small boat with just one fisherman docked. The boat had several large fresh fish in it.

The investment banker was impressed by the quality of the fish and asked the Mexican how long it took to catch them.

The Mexican replied: "Only a little while."

The banker then asked why he did not stay out longer to catch more fish.

The fisherman replied he had enough to support his family's immediate needs.

The American then asked: "But what do you do with the rest of your time?"

The fisherman replied: "I sleep late, fish a little, play with my children, take siesta with my wife, stroll into the village each evening where I sip wine and play guitar with my amigos. I have a full and busy life, señor."

The investment banker scoffed a little and said "I am an Ivy League MBA and I could help you. You could spend more time fishing and with the proceeds buy a bigger boat. With the proceeds from the bigger boat, you could buy several boats until eventually you would have a whole fleet of fishing boats. Instead of selling your catch to the middleman, you could sell directly to the processor, eventually opening your own cannery. You could control the product, processing and distribution."

He then added: "Of course, you would need to leave this small coastal fishing village and move to Mexico City where you would run your growing enterprise."

The Mexican fisherman asked “But señor, how long will this all take?”

To which the American replied “15-20 years.”

“But what then?” asked the Mexican.

The American laughed and said “That’s the best part. When the time is right you would announce an IPO and sell your company stock to the public and become very rich. You could make millions.”

“Millions, señor? Then what?”

To which the investment banker replied “Then you would retire. You could move to a small coastal fishing village where you would sleep late, fish a little, play with your kids, take siesta with your wife, stroll to the village in the evenings where you could sip wine and play your guitar with your amigos.”

You see, just like the Mexican, it is important you know what your aims are so that you can make sure your business goals align.

Business goals

Now set your one-year and three-year business goals of how you're going to achieve these. This might be increasing turnover by x amount or recruiting new staff.

Once you've set your goals, you can formulate an action plan as to how you're going to achieve them.

I have a large whiteboard in my office. On the right side I have my yearly goals, covering everything I wish to achieve in that particular year. On the left side I have my monthly, smaller goals. That is everything I'm going to do that month to help achieve my yearly goals.

The whiteboard is the first thing I see every day when I come into the office and it helps me get focused straight away.

Company vision

When you start your new company, it's important to have formulated your company vision. What is your end goal? Where do you visualise your company going?

Our company vision for *Non Stop Kids Entertainment* was:

- To be a national company and a well-known brand across the UK;
- To provide the best in entertainment and customer service; and
- To always put the customer first to provide the best service possible.

It is really important to have a clear vision and to know it off by heart for several reasons.

The first is that it reminds you of what you're trying to achieve. Sometimes opportunities will arise and as an entrepreneur it is tempting to take any opportunity that comes your way. However, you need to stop and think whether this is going to contribute to your end game? Does this help and does it fit in with your company vision?

For example, we had a tempting proposal to team up with a well-respected entertainment agency, offering us the promise of lots of parties, but we had to deliver the entertainment under their brand.

Well it was a great opportunity and meant we could get lots of work. However, it was going to tie up most of our team and it went against our vision of becoming a well-known brand in our own right.

I probably wouldn't have thought of that if I hadn't figured out what our vision was.

The second reason is that it keeps you accountable to yourself. In my case it might be: "Yeah sure we can probably pull the wool over the customers' eyes and get away with it." But did that fit our company vision about always putting the customer first?

Well no, it didn't; and nor would it help our vision to provide the best possible service.

Thirdly, and probably most importantly, when it comes to bringing in new members of staff, you should be able to sell the company to them on your vision alone. This is what we are about! This is what we are going to achieve and maintain! Then everyone who works for you should be on the same page. The goals and strategies might change, but everyone is pulling in the same direction because they all share the vision.

Chapter 4 – Establish The Right Systems And Procedures

It is important when you start out on your own that you create a business and not just a job for yourself.

There is a massive difference between the two. Initially, you will probably have to work very hard to get everything done.

In his book, "*Life: Business Just Got Easier*", Brad Burton says: 'The best thing about being self-employed is you get to choose which 18 hours a day you work.' That is true.

When you start, you have to do everything yourself. This includes planning and strategy, finance and accounting, legal issues, marketing and sales, customer service, human resources and the actual service your business provides to its customers.

Nigel Botterill, a successful entrepreneur here in the UK, describes it like this. Imagine there is a man named James who wants to play football (soccer). He has a look at different leagues and teams online and joins a Sunday League team near his house.

He buys all the equipment and turns up for his first match, quite excited and feeling ready to face the world.

The other team looks quite professional and he is starting to feel out of his depth. The referee blows the whistle. The match kicks off. James realises there is only one of him and the other team has a full complement of 11 players on the pitch. He has started in the goalkeeper position, so the other team is passing around with ease. He runs out to defence to try to make a challenge, but it's no good.

After just a few minutes the other team is basically out of sight and James is exhausted, deflated and feeling completely beaten.

Now in real life that would never happen. No one would attempt to take on a football team with 11 players, but that is what happens in business all the time.

So how do we overcome this huge problem?

Manage your time wisely. Systemise and eliminate.

Most people at work waste time and lots of it. It's more important to work smart than to work hard. Of course, if you can do both even better.

Early in my working life this time management tool was shared with me and I have found it to be extremely useful over the years.

	Urgent	Not Urgent
Important		
Not Important		

What I would like you to do is to make a list of all the tasks that you have to do in your job. Once you have made the list, put each task inside one of the boxes above.

Top left is for tasks that are Urgent **and** Important.

Top right is for tasks that are Important but Not Urgent.

Bottom left is for tasks that are Urgent but Not Important.

And bottom right is for tasks that are Not Important **and** Not Urgent.

Once you've placed all the tasks in the correct boxes, I suggest everything in the top left is going to take priority because those tasks are Important **and** Urgent.

It's very easy when you first get into work to do non urgent tasks, such as checking emails and putting off doing the tasks that really need to get done – the important and urgent tasks.

Everything in the bottom right includes the tasks which are not urgent and are also not important, so eliminate them!

You are wasting your time if you are doing these tasks.

The other two boxes are the interesting ones. The tasks here still need to be done as they are either important or urgent – but do you need to be the one that does them?
They are the ones I would recommend either systemising or getting someone else to do. You can outsource these if you don't have any members of staff.

I will give you an example of an item in my to-do list which I put in the Urgent but Not Important box and decided to outsource.

Answering the telephone can seriously interrupt your work and meetings. My solution was to hire a virtual assistant to answer calls for me. My productivity doubled over the following few weeks.

It is really important that you study each task to make sure that it is in the right box.

I will give you another example. A few months ago, I was talking to a young lady called Hannah. She is a business owner and also one of my advanced students.

Hannah was complaining about the amount of printing and filing she had to do. It was taking her one to two hours per day – about eight hours every week.

I asked Hannah if, instead of printing out documents, she could save them straight onto her computer. She explained that her accountant insisted on doing it this way as, in the unlikely event of HM Revenue & Customs ever investigating her company, all her documentation would need to be printed out.

I didn't believe her. I believed she believed it, but surely HMRC would be happy to view everything digitally? I decided to investigate. I called HMRC and sure enough saving documents straight onto your computer is absolutely fine.

She believed that printing and filing was Important but Not Urgent, whereas it was actually Not Important and Not

Urgent. So what did she do when she realised? You guessed it. Hannah eliminated it.

Eliminate everything you can. If you can't eliminate it, systemise it. If you can't systemise it, get someone else to do it for you. That is the goal.

What do I mean by systemise?

We live in an amazing era, with the internet and fantastic computer software. Take advantage of that to help your business.

I will give you a couple of examples of systems that we have used to help our business. The biggest and best example is a CRM system. CRM stands for customer relationship management and wow they can be incredible! A good CRM system will offer email marketing and a sales platform for small businesses, including products to streamline the customer life-cycle, customer relationship management, marketing automation, lead capture and e-commerce. Now I know these are just the features of what a CRM system can do, so let me practice what I preach and give you some examples of how it can benefit your business.

When I ran my entertainment company we used a CRM to:

> Chase clients for deposits and balance payments. This on its own saves hours every week. The CRM software will email and text clients, reminding them to pay until they do. Eventually it stops chasing them. This is automatic and we're only advised that a client has not paid after the CRM has decided to cancel the entertainment at their event.
>
> Send confirmation emails and follow up. A member of our sales team fills in one form and then the CRM will add the booking onto our main booking system. It will also email the entertainer all the details they

require (name and address of client, details of the event etc.) and add them to their calendar; email a confirmation email to the customer; send follow-up information to the client via text and email, with useful party information and FAQs.

I could go on.

CRMs have saved us countless hours over the years and the more your business grows, the more time it will save you.

You can also systemise your social media on platforms such as Facebook, Instagram and LinkedIn by using scheduling software, or even better by hiring a digital marketer to distribute your content. You can film a 10 minute video to publish on YouTube, which could be filmed using your smart phone and then ask your assistant to turn that 10 minute video into micro content. 1 video could easily be turned into:

1 x Blog
3 x Quotes
3 x 1 min smaller / teaser videos

Suddenly your one video has given you a week's worth of social media content.

Make sure you implement these changes into your business as soon as possible. Put them in your Urgent and Important box. You will thank me in the long run.

Get a great team around you

In our football team analogy, we saw how it can be very difficult to make it on your own. The biggest piece of advice I can give is to not be afraid of employing staff.

Many business owners are not prepared to take this step. They are worried about getting stuck with a bad employee or getting sued. Unless you take the big step of employing people, it is going to be very hard to grow a successful and, more importantly, saleable business.

I have made mistakes when hiring staff. I have taken on the wrong individuals, but like anything, the more you do it the better you will get. I once employed someone in a sales role who could certainly sell. This was the only thing I really focused on in the interview as I believed the rest of the job would be easy for him.

However, he continually made admin errors, some of them rather costly, and could not use his own initiative. I felt like I was working almost as hard babysitting him. It was as if I was doing all the work myself. Sadly, we had to let him go. You win some you lose some, but just make sure when you lose you learn from it and don't make the same mistake again. The next person we hired went on to become a successful manager.

Always start an employee on a six-month probation period. This means that if you have made a mistake and they are the wrong person for the job, like we did, or even your company can no longer afford to pay their wages, it is easier and cheaper to dismiss them during these six months. It is standard practice to restrict notice periods to just one week during probationary periods. The best advice is always to be fair and transparent with employees, treat them with respect, don't discriminate and be upfront about their capabilities, and your business needs, so that when it doesn't work out, you can let them go with a clear conscience.

Probably half of our staff at the moment are people I knew before I started the company. This is great because if you know them personally, you tend to know their strengths and weaknesses. I always look for people who are team players, have a good, hard-working attitude and are intelligent. If they have these qualities, you will be able to train them to do the job and they will excel.

If you are not in a position to hire any staff, start by outsourcing. Use the time management tool that we used earlier to decide which tasks you would like to farm out. You can meet virtual assistants and accountants at networking groups such as 4Networking, or by asking other small businesses if they are happy to recommend the companies they use.

Organisational structure

When your business begins to grow, and you start to have different people (employees or outsourced staff) engaged in different tasks, it is your responsibility to ensure that everyone knows what they should be doing and that everything gets done.

Using a strong organisational structure allows everyone in your enterprise to work together as a team. It means that each person knows exactly what their job role is and helps your workforce to pull together in the same direction.

I suggest creating an organisational structure that everyone has access to; make people responsible for different tasks so that no one can say: 'Oh I didn't do that, I thought Sally would have taken care of it.'

You can edit this regularly as you expand. It should look something like this:

	MD	
	(Name of MD s/he answers to the board)	
Sales and Marketing	**Operations**	**Support**
(Name of Sales and Marketing Manager)	(Name of Operations Manager)	(Name of Support Manager)
List of all marketing activities eg	List of all Operations activities eg.	List of all Support activities
Direct Sales	Delivery the product	HR
Marketing	Production	Finance
Developments		Receptionist
Key Performance Indicator Eg	**Key Performance Indicator Eg**	**Key Performance Indicator Eg**
1. Meeting Sales Targets	1. Few Returns	1. Sufficent Happy Staff
2. Generating Sufficient Leads	2. Satisfied Customers	2. Accounts Ready on Time
		3. Payroll Paid on Time
		4. Complaints / Problems dealt with

Begin by making a list of all the activities that need to be performed to run your business and place them under the appropriate category e.g. sales and marketing.

Next, you must assign the name of the person responsible for making sure the task actually gets done. This means that there are no questions asked or fingers pointed if anything goes wrong.

Once you have done this, assign your sales and marketing, operations and support services managers. It is their responsibility to ensure that all the tasks get done.

When you first get started every role will most likely be filled by you, but as you grow and hire staff, or outsource, you continually update your organisational structure with the names of the people who are taking responsibility for those tasks.

Your job as Managing Director is to oversee everything. You can do this through regular weekly, monthly and quarterly meetings and by examining your key performance indicators. Are you, for example, hitting your sales targets?

When can you fire yourself?

It may seem like a strange question, but that is what I ask myself when starting a new business.

My ultimate goal in any business is that I'm able to fire myself as soon as possible. As soon as you are no longer needed in the day-to-day running of the business, you have successfully created a passive income. You are now being paid for doing NOTHING.

This frees up your time to do whatever you want to do, whether that is travelling the world or, in my case, setting up further businesses as that is what I love to do.

In his brilliant book, "*The 4 Hour Work Week*", Tim Ferriss points out that it is strange that people work really hard all of their lives with the end goal being retirement. The problem is that retirement is when you are likely to be past your prime to enjoy it.

If you can create a business where you can fire yourself, you can enjoy mini retirements all the way along. You can travel the world, spend time with your children as they grow up, play golf or do whatever you desire.

The point is that if you're not needed in your company for its day-to-day running, it gives you options to focus on other things. That is why it is always my ultimate goal.

Chapter 5 - Total Market Domination

Be honest, everyone would like to dominate their market. If you want to boss your industry, you need to make your sales and marketing the best in that field.

I say sales and marketing, but it should be the other way round, because the marketing comes first and then the sales.

Some people get the two confused, so to be clear: marketing consists of generating leads which includes any activity that would cause someone to be interested in your product. Sales involves getting that interested person to actually buy from you.

In this chapter, we're going to look at marketing techniques and more specifically the three-step plan which I have used to successfully dominate the market.

1. - Have a great product

If you want to dominate your market, it doesn't matter how good your marketing is, or how good you are at sales, you will get found out if you have a poor product.

When I first started as an entertainer, my product was me and, unfortunately, I had an inferior product.

Before the heady days of *Slightly Unusual*, when Craig Petty and I were performing on ITV and SKY TV, as well as winning awards, we were a double act. We advertised ourselves as comedy-magicians, but we had two problems.

The first one was that we were not funny and the second was that our tricks sometimes went wrong. I will always remember the first cabaret show we ever did.

Craig called me and said: 'I've just had a phone call from a chap called Danny who runs a comedy club in Nottingham. Danny wants to book something a little bit different for his next comedy night. He wants us to do 15 minutes to finish the first half of his show and then another 15 minutes to finish the second half. What do you think?'

'I'm not sure, do you think we can do it?' I replied.

'Well, I've said yes, so we're going to have to,' said Craig.

So although we were marketing ourselves, we didn't even have an act ready yet. Luckily, we had four weeks before the big day to plan, prepare and assemble our act.

As it turned out, we met up the day before the gig, at Craig's house, to start preparing and planning.

When we arrived at the venue, Danny bounded over excitedly and greeted us at the door. He explained that he was going to be filming the whole show and putting it on the internet. That added to the pressure.

We were quite nervous and felt a bit under prepared but were still confident the show would go well.

All of the acts before us were really funny and the audience was loving it. Craig and I were just looking at each other and, although we didn't say anything, we were both thinking OMG we are going to die.

After what seemed like forever, we were eventually introduced on stage.

We ran out onto the stage and Craig was holding a large brown envelope with a question mark drawn on it with a permanent marker pen.

We asked a member of the audience to name any celebrity.

'Tom Cruise,' they said.

I then announced that Craig had been holding a large envelope the entire time and inside we had a picture of Tom Cruise. Craig then pulled out the picture shouting 'aged six months' as he pulled out a generic picture of a six-month-old baby.

Silence. You could almost see tumbleweed blowing across the stage.

This audience which had been laughing loudly throughout the other acts did not find us funny.

We hurriedly moved onto our next trick. We had actually created this trick ourselves and it was all based on the lottery. Two members of the audience would join us on stage. The first then fills in a lottery slip with their chosen numbers. I would then go backstage to get the balls for the second audience member to draw randomly out of a bag. And 'ta-da,' they would match. Well at least in theory.

Without revealing the method when I went backstage, I would know the numbers that the first person had picked. I would then place the balls in such a way that the second person would pick the balls which matched the first volunteer's choices. Clever right?

So we start the routine and everything is going to plan. It is now time for me to go backstage and get the balls. I disappear backstage but the vital information is not there.

I'm desperately looking around knowing that without this there is no trick, but I can't find anything. So I decided to just not go back out.

After a few moments of awkward silence Craig shouts: 'Russ have you got the balls?'

'No!' I shout back.

'Well, where are they?' Craig asks.

'I don't know,' is all I can think to reply.

Safe to say it was not a good first half. Danny approached us during the interval and said:

'Instead of doing 15 minutes to close the second half, could you guys just do five minutes at the beginning. Also, you might notice that I'm not filming you. It's because we're running low on film.'

That might have been more believable if he had not spent the rest of the interval filming people just messing around.

So we ran back on stage to start the second half. We needed to bring up another volunteer to assist us and Craig asked him to seal an envelope. The line I was to deliver just after he sealed it was:

'That's funny, it didn't stick when I licked it earlier!'

This led to boos of disapproval from the audience as a weak gag. Even Craig who had written the line was embarrassed. He turned to me and said:

'Russ, that's the worst joke I've ever heard!'

We finished our five minutes and left the stage utterly humiliated. What came next was even worse.

The next act to appear on stage was a freestyle rapper named DJ Wheezey. While we were sitting depressed on the sidelines, he spent his entire slot rapping about how rubbish Craig and I had been. The audience, of course, lapped it up.

We drove home from Nottingham that night in complete silence. Neither of us said a word.

The problem was with our product. It didn't matter how effectively we marketed ourselves, as soon as someone saw us, we would not be invited back. We spent the rest of the year constantly rehearsing, performing for free and studying other successful acts so that we had a great product which we could market successfully.

So be honest with yourself. Do you have a product that you would be proud to sell to your friends and family? If you do, read on. And if not, make sure to work on your product until you do.

2. - Positioning

When you're planning on marketing a product or a service, you need to know where you're going to position yourself in the market. All the big companies, such as Disney and McDonalds, do this and you should too.

So who is it that you're marketing your product to?

There are three different types of people you might want to consider marketing to. The first is the group I like to call the Cheapskates. These are the people who just like to spend the least amount of money possible. They will shop around gathering quotes and will not take quality into account. They just want the product at the lowest possible price.

There are a whole variety of reasons why someone might be in the Cheapskate category when it comes to buying your product or service. It might be that they don't value what you do, or maybe they literally can't afford any more. Just because someone is a Cheapskate when it comes to buying your product does not mean they will be for all products. You might have someone who lives in a really nice house and drives a really nice car but is a Cheapskate when it comes, for example, to booking a children's entertainer.

If a Cheapskate were buying a car, they would probably look on a website such as AutoTrader to buy a second-hand car that was going for about £500 and wouldn't really be overly concerned about the make or model of the car.

Obviously, percentages vary from industry to industry but typically about 25 percent of any market is made up of Cheapskates.

The second group of people are the Value For Money people. These are the people who want a good service and are happy to pay for it. They will also shop around and compare quotes but, unlike their Cheapskate counterparts, they'll examine price and quality to find that happy medium. Chances are you sit somewhere in the Value For Money camp as they make up 68 percent of the market. If someone from this category were going to buy a car, it could vary greatly depending on their budget and whether they wanted to buy a new or second-hand car. However, they would probably read reviews and examine factors like fuel economy, reliability, resale value and build quality. They would then most probably go on to buy a model like a Ford or a Honda.

The final group I call Premium. Premium is the smallest group, making up just seven percent of the market. The clue is in the name. Premium customers want to pay for a premium product. They want the absolute best and are happy to pay a premium price. There are hotels that charge $100,000 per night. That is insane. You could stay at a decent four-star hotel for £100.

In fact, sometimes it is the high price that attracts the Premium group. The fact they know most people will not be able to afford it makes it extra special.

So which market should you aim your product at?

In my opinion, you should avoid aiming it at the Cheapskates. If people are purchasing from you, based solely on price, it means you're going to have disloyal customers –
customers who as soon as someone else is slightly cheaper will leave you in a heartbeat. This leaves you with two options: either you lose your customers, or you drop your prices to compete. This will impact your profit margins. Not good.

The other issue with Cheapskates is that they always tend to want something for nothing and they're quick to complain and find fault.

Having said that, there are certain situations where you might want to target Cheapskates. For instance, if you're selling in vast bulk and are happy to make a small profit on each transaction. It is not, however, an option that I have ever explored for the reasons given above.

My children's entertainment company, *Non Stop Kids Entertainment*, had a large team of entertainers. We wanted to book in as many parties as possible to fulfil our goals and company vision. As a brief reminder, these were:

> 'To be a national company and a well-known brand across the UK, providing the best in entertainment, and always putting the customer first to provide the best service possible.'

For this reason, *Non Stop Kids Entertainment* targeted the Value For Money customers. First, it has by far the biggest market share and also it allowed us to charge a fair price for providing a quality service.

We were more expensive than some, but not all, children's entertainers. Our customers bought into our brand. They liked our website with our young and energetic entertainers and, when they contacted us, they appreciated our great customer service.

They saw a quality service throughout the whole booking process and during the delivery. For this reason, they were happy to pay a fair price for the service. After all, it was their little darlings' special day. They wanted it to be exciting and memorable.

As you know, our other entertainment company was called *Slightly Unusual*. We essentially copied the *Non Stop Kids Entertainment* business model onto *Slightly Unusual,* but as things stood, there was a big difference between *Slightly Unusual* and *Non Stop Kids*.

Slightly Unusual was an act and not an agency, and I was a performer in that act. That meant that when a client booked *Slightly Unusual*, I had to go there myself. So, unlike *Non Stop Kids*, my focus was not on booking in as many gigs as possible because I only had so much time that I could put into performing.

With *Slightly Unusual,* therefore, we targeted the Premium customers so that we could get as well paid for our time as possible. Now if you want to target the Premium market it is vital that the look of your brand, your marketing, your website and even your pricing are premium too. It is important to gather as much social proof as possible to attract those Premium customers. You can afford to go the extra mile and throw in nice little surprises that make your clients feel special because your profit margin is much higher.

Once you have decided which market sector you want to position yourself in, it is important you know exactly who that is.

3. - Who?

When you are starting out, you need to establish what exactly you are selling and your target audience.

Who are the people that sit in this market? Where do they go? What do they look for? When do they buy? What do they want?

This will require research. If you are already an established business, you can start by analysing your clientele. The best way I have found to do this is to email all your previous customers, promising them a free gift or entry into a prize draw if they complete a short survey which you have designed to profile your customers. Not everyone will fill this in, but if you provide a compelling incentive you should receive sufficient responses to provide you with the data you need.

If you don't have a list of customers, try to research other companies which offer similar services to what you plan on offering. This can be tricky and might require some guesswork at first until you can start building the data.

One other great trick is that if you see a competitor's paid advertisement on Facebook there will be a little downwards arrow in the top right-hand corner. If you click on this arrow, a tab bar will appear. Click on 'Why Am I Seeing This Ad.' It will then tell you why they are targeting you. It may be gender, age etc.

Once you have done this, it gives you some clues as to who you should be targeting.

When we performed the short survey task for *Non Stop Kids Entertainment,* we found out that most of our customers were:

- Female
- Had children
- Were aged between 25 and 40
- Had at least one child between four and eight
- Had a household income of £30,000 per year +
- Used social media every day

So when we designed a website or crafted an advert, these were the people we wanted to attract.

You need to put yourself in their shoes or ask your friends, who fit their profile, questions such as:

> Where would you look if you decided you wanted to hire an entertainer for your child's birthday?
>
> What do you think of the advert I've written?

Once you have a clear picture in your head of who you want to sell your product to, it helps to keep your branding consistent, such as your logo and your website. It also enables you to implement marketing strategies which will directly target the correct audience.

This is especially useful if you decide to use Facebook adverts. Facebook knows everything about you; how much you earn, how much you spend, where you live, where your family lives, if you have children etc.

This is terrible news if you are a private person, but great if you have an audience that you have profiled and want to market to. So be sure to look into Facebook ads, if you believe your audience is on Facebook.

Chapter 6 - Marketing Activities You Need to Implement

Hopefully by now you have a clear idea of who you want to market to. Marketing has evolved. Gone are the days when you could put an advert in the Yellow Pages or in a local newspaper and the telephone would not stop ringing.

One of the most effective ways of marketing is to not advertise at all. Instead you need to **Give Value** to your potential customers.

You can create blogs, videos and articles that your target market would find interesting instead of a traditional advert.

I'll give you an example about the letting agency we bought, *Quick Move.* We wanted to target landlords.

The more landlords we had, the more properties we had to let out. So, rather than creating a traditional advert, we produced a series of videos on how landlords can make more money from their properties. We then distributed these videos for free on social media. This is exactly the sort of information that active landlords want to be given.

All they have to do is provide us with their email address and they automatically get sent a video every week.

It is useful information to them and at some point during the video we would mention how important it is for them to have a top letting agency such as *Quick Move*.

If they're looking for, or thinking of changing letting agents, who do you think they're going to call?

Google has become a household name by giving customers value for free. Think along the lines of the Google search function, Google Maps, Google Drive and Gmail.

So I strongly suggest you give careful consideration to what you can give your clients for free? Is it information that sets you up as an expert?

Videos are an excellent way of showcasing what you can offer. They let your potential clients get to know you, your company and what you are all about.

When I worked in entertainment, it was very easy for my two companies, *Non Stop Kids Entertainment* and *Slightly Unusual*, to create video content. Both businesses revolved around entertainment, so people were interested in viewing the content.

I put a video on Facebook of me cheating at cards with the classic gambling game 'Chase the Ace' and it got over 35,000 views in a couple of weeks.

However, it does not have to be visual. I tried to think of the most boring profession and came up with accounting. Apologies to any accountants reading this book!

One of my favourite gags is: 'Why don't accountants look out of the window in the morning? Because they'd have nothing to do in the afternoon.'

Sorry, I'm getting distracted now. I searched on Google for how to set up QuickBooks
(QuickBooks is an accountancy/bookkeeping software package). The top search result returned a video that had more than one million views and over 2,500 likes. Yet it looked really basic and boring to me.

So this just goes to prove that whatever your field, e.g. entertainment or accountancy, if people are interested in what you have to offer, videos are fantastic advertising for your company, especially if you provide value in the video - that takes it to another level of marketing.

The point is that you do not necessarily have to have fancy equipment and editing skills to make a massive impact. Just a simple video, shot on a smartphone, that you can upload to social media and share, can attract a huge audience.

Sometimes the videos will work brilliantly, and you get loads of views. However, this doesn't always happen. I've been convinced that I've come up with the best video idea ever, only for it to get 500 views. At other times, like with the 'Chase the Ace' video, I was expecting 500 views and it got thousands. The key is to keep creating lots of content and get your company name out there as much as you can.

Make sure that all your adverts and content have **a clear call to action at the end.**

A call to action means asking the prospect to do something at the end of the video, blog, or article. Common calls to action include Call Now, Buy Now, Click Here For More. There is no point creating a fantastic video that gets 10,000 views if no one knows who you are, where you're from and what you want them to do.

So, if you were the accountant who created the 'How to set up QuickBooks' video you might insert a call to action at the end, such as:

> 'If you want an expert to set up your QuickBooks account for you, call 0800 xxxx xxx today for a no-obligation quote.'

This will then be seen by one million people who want to open a QuickBooks account, but unless you tell them what you want them to do, nothing will happen.

One of my favourite marketing techniques is **Social Proof.** Social proof is anything that makes you sound or look good to prospective clients. This could be awards, impressive sounding clients, newspaper articles, TV appearances, good reviews, being part of a respected trade union or organisation.

When we set up our illusion act *Slightly Unusual,* we wanted to target premium customers. We knew that to stand out from the crowd we needed to generate as much social proof as possible.

This was our mission, so we spent about two years entering every competition that we could, applying for TV shows, performing at showcases and fringe festivals for free, asking anyone who watched our act to give us a video testimonial.

Performing at the Brighton Fringe was an interesting experience. We had 12 shows booked over a two-week period, so it was quite intense. The accommodation in Brighton was expensive due to the high demand brought about by the fringe festival. So we stayed about an hour's drive away in a static caravan. That way we also had a kitchen as we figured it would be cheaper to buy food rather than eating out all the time.

We spent the days walking around the streets of Brighton handing out flyers and calling newspapers and agents to see if they wanted complimentary tickets to our show. It was hard work and we only sold about 20-30 tickets a night. This meant that we actually made a loss of about £1,000 over the two weeks, taking into consideration the accommodation, venue hire, flyers, newspaper advert, food and everything else involved.

However, we got the following review from a well-known magazine:

> *'Slightly Unusual is a brilliant and exciting comical illusion act. The show comprises laughter, magic, gags, sleight of hand tricks and major illusions to*

> *produce an hour of fun. The guys are fantastic, enthusiastic and very talented. The speed at which they execute the illusions just adds to the wow factor and makes the impossible happen in front of your very eyes.'*

We also clinched a year-long contract from an agent, performing at holiday parks across the UK, which was worth more than £80,000, and generated a huge number of video testimonials.

So it was great social proof and well worth the hard two weeks.

Over that two-year period, we also got fantastic reviews from *The Stage* newspaper, we performed on ITV1 and Sky TV. We won accolades, such as the *British Magical Society Magicians of the Year* and *Brit Idol Public Choice Award*, and had hundreds of video testimonials. Our client list was impressive too. It included celebrities and large corporations.

All this social proof provides powerful marketing content that you can share. It also places you head and shoulders above your competitors when customers are comparing quotes.

What should I do?

There are lots of different marketing activities that work. There is no right or wrong answer. I have found that some will work in one industry and then entirely flop in another.

You will need to put yourself in the shoes of your client. Where would you look if you were them? Then try it to test the data so you can analyse what does and doesn't work.

To help you make your mind up as to what would work best for your business, I'm going to give you a brief summary of some of the marketing strategies that have worked for me over the years.

Website: no matter what industry you're in, you need a good website. Scratch that. You need a great website.

Some people say to me: 'No one in my industry has a website so I don't think I need one.'
If no one in your industry has a website, even more reason to have one. It will allow you to stand out from your competition, and if anyone looks for your service or products online you will be the one who shows up.

You can hire a professional to build a website for you or you can build your own one, using software such as WordPress or Wix. This is an easy way to build a website without having to understand how to code. It is certainly a lot cheaper but can be time-consuming. However, if you don't know what you're doing, your site could look rather shoddy or amateurish.

In this day and age, your website is your main marketing tool, so make sure that it is simple to use. It should be designed to get sales, so avoid loading it full of useless information.

Before you start the design work of the website, whether you are doing it yourself or getting a professional to do it for you, map out all the pages you want. Once you know this, get all the text written for those pages.

If you don't think you can write interesting content, you might want to consider getting a copywriter to produce the text for you.

Then make sure you've got plenty of eye-catching photographs to make the website look appealing. These do not need to be high resolution images if you're only using them online. Smartphones are so good nowadays. Lots of the images on my websites were taken on my phone.

AdWords vs SEO - What are they and what is the difference?

They are both ways to get your website showing up on a search engine (usually Google) when people are looking for the terms relevant to your business.

With AdWords, you write an advertisement and pay Google to display it when certain words are searched for by a potential customer. You only pay if and when that potential customer clicks on the advert and arrives on your website.

For example, if someone searched for 'children's entertainer Birmingham' on Google our advert for Non Stop Kids Entertainment would appear. We would only pay for that if the person clicked on our ad.

The more popular the search terms, the more you have to bid to appear at the top of the search engine results. Google changes how it displays adverts but currently it shows about three at the top of the page and another three at the bottom. Google will then repeat this on the next few pages.

The more you bid on a keyword the higher you will show up. Obviously if you are at the bottom of page two, it is highly unlikely that your advert will get clicked on, compared to one at the top of page one.

This means that if you want more clicks you will have to bid a higher amount than your competitors to show higher than them. Google will tell you how much you need to bid to appear on the first page.

You can choose as many or as few keywords as you want and can bid a different amount for each one.

To control your spend, you set a daily budget so that you cannot get hundreds of clicks and accidently spend hundreds or thousands of pounds.

So, for example, you might have 15 search terms each with a maximum bid of £1 per click and with a maximum daily spend of £20.

You can also limit the number and quality of clicks that you get by only allowing your advert to show in certain areas and at certain times.

Among the best and most useful tools are negative keywords. Negative keywords are words in the search term that you do not like. If someone puts one of these words into their search term your advert will not show.

You might be an electrician who lives in Birmingham and has 'electrician in Birmingham' as a keyword. So if someone searched 'cheap electrician in Birmingham,' your advert would be displayed.

But that might be useless to you as you are not cheap, and you target the premium market. So now you are having to pay for this person to click on your website and quickly realise that you are not the electrician for them.

However, if you added the word 'cheap' to your negative keywords your advert would not have shown up.

Google will actually show you all the different search terms used by people who then go on to click on your advert. This means that you can look through the list and add any of the terms you dislike to your negative keywords.

AdWords is not the sort of marketing that you can just set up and leave unattended. You will constantly need to monitor it, add more keywords, as well as change your bids and adverts. You may wish to do this yourself or outsource it to someone who knows what they're doing.

Google is also helpful when you are setting up the campaign and will be happy to walk you through it over the phone.

SEO stands for Search Engine Optimisation. This allows you to show up organically, without having to pay, as with AdWords. It is much more difficult to appear organically and there are lots of ever-changing factors that come into play when Google decides who to show first. The most important thing you can do to help your website rank highly is to create a site that is full of well written, interesting and unique content – content that your potential customers will search for and enjoy reading. It takes time before you start showing up and it is probably worth hiring a professional to help if you are serious about ranking at the top.

Social media

Even if you are not technologically savvy, it is really important that you have a strong presence on social media. Everyone is on social media these days, so it is the perfect platform to promote and advertise your business. In many cases you can do it for free. How great is that?

Here are the main reasons I use social media in my businesses.

It builds trust

If you have an active page, it helps to build trust before the customer actually buys from you.

Anyone can put on their website whatever they want, telling people how brilliant they are. But with the amount of fraud online, people are often dubious about paying for a product or service just because you say you are great.

If you are active and engaging on social media, potential clients can see how you interact with existing customers. They can read reviews and see your company in action on videos that you have shared. It proves you are a real company and shows them how you do business. People can also see the standard of work that you provide.

Improves your client retention

One of the biggest benefits of having an engaging social media page is that, once someone likes your page and sees all your blogs, posts and videos, it keeps your business at the forefront of their minds.

Let's say you booked *Slightly Unusual* to perform their award-winning illusion show at your wedding. They came along and did an awesome job. All your guests loved it and at the time you liked their Facebook page. Every day you are on Facebook and quite often you see interesting blogs, videos and posts by *Slightly Unusual*.

Two years later you get asked to hire the entertainment for your company's Christmas party. *Slightly Unusual* are going to be the first company that comes to mind, rather than thinking: 'who was that act we hired two years ago?' . And that's because you see them regularly on social media.

Drives traffic to your website

When people are reading your blogs and watching your videos make sure you include a link for them to visit your website. The more interesting and valuable content you provide, the more people are going to be clicking on your website. This in turn leads to more sales. It really is a no brainer.

Provides great customer service

As we know, people use social media all the time. If you have a page and they message you, whether to buy from you or ask a question, they will expect a response.

It is important that you, or whoever checks your social media, responds quickly to allow you to provide the great customer service that you would expect if a client rang or emailed you.

Allows you to keep an eye on the competition

It is easy to keep track of your competitors on social media, to see what blogs they are writing and whether they have any special offers. This can be very useful in giving you ideas to help grow your business.

If you are not the sort of person who can manage your own social media campaign, it may be worth hiring a pro to do it for you. Make sure, however, that you understand your objectives and play a part in the blogs (or any other promotional material), even if you do not write them yourself.

A cheaper way, although it does require a bit more work, is to use the specific software like Edgar, Hootsuite or equivalent.

They're fantastic tools to help you post regularly and also recycle plenty of the material you create. The advantage of this is that you are not having to create fresh content all the time. Also, remember that not all the content has to be unique. There is nothing wrong with sharing posts on your page that are relevant and interesting. It doesn't all have to be about selling your product to provide value.

Facebook ads

Facebook is a great place to market your business and Facebook ads give you a very clever way of targeting the right person.

In the Total Market Domination chapter, we look at how you should know the identity of your customers. Once you know your customer's identity, Facebook will allow you to just show your ads to the exact type of people who buy from you.

Facebook knows everything about you, from where you live, who your relatives are and where they live, to where you shop and eat, what your political views are, how much you earn and what your interests are – in fact pretty much everything about you.

This is pretty bad news if you are a private person and like the idea of data protection. However, if you're looking to market your business to a particular type of person it's gold dust.

When you create your advert on Facebook, you must then pick the exact type of person you want to see it. You can choose what they're into, how much money they earn, if they have children etc.

So think about just how powerful that can be.

Networking

Particularly when you start out in business, networking is a great way to get new clients but also a great chance to buy from other people and make contacts.

There is more to networking than just marketing, so don't expect to get results straight away. It's about building relationships and this can take time.

There is a saying in networking that it is all about:

Know, like, trust.

You first get to know people; you then get to like them and finally you begin to trust them. Only then are you ready to buy from them. It might take six months before you get your first sale from regularly attending a networking meeting.

Too often people try to network for a month or two and then quit because it 'didn't work,' but they haven't given people enough time to get to know, like and trust them.

It's like when you start going to the gym. It takes time before you see any results at all. If someone went to the gym once or twice and said: 'Wow that didn't work, I don't have a six pack yet,' you would think they were crazy. Networking is exactly the same.

Here are some tips that have worked for me when networking:

1. Do not go into the room just thinking only about selling your product. If you are open to other people and listen to what they have to offer, they are more likely to be open to listening to you.

2. Do not expect results straight away. Instead, work on building relationships and make sure everyone knows exactly what you do and who your customers are.

3. Be consistent. Don't be the person who attends 10 meetings in their first month and then disappears for the next six months. As with most things, consistency is key.

4. Get a great 60 seconds. At most networking meetings you will have an opportunity to tell everyone in the room exactly what you do.

In my eyes, almost more important than going to a set networking group is just to always be networking in real life – always asking people what they do, building relationships and being on the lookout for opportunities at church, on the school run, at the gym, in the coffee shop, or wherever it is you go.

Most of my staff have been hired as a result of real-life networking. My right-hand man in the office, and operations manager of our training business, was called Jack. I met him at church and got to know him well. I thought this guy is efficient, hard-working, loyal and a good people person, so I offered him a job.

Our top sales guy in the office was Elliot. I went to school with him. My PA was Abbie, my cousin's girlfriend. I could go on, but I think you get the point.

Once you tap into someone's network you could get loads of work as a result of recommendations. Our training company gets about 20 percent of its clients from people using us and then recommending us to friends and family. So, make sure people know what you do; that you have a damn good product or service and deliver on your promises.

Blogs

Blogging can be a very powerful way of building yourself a reputation as an expert and providing useful content to the people in your target market who may buy from you. It can also help you appear high in Google search results.

I'll give you an example. I just searched on Google for things to do in Birmingham.

One of the top links that appeared was '21 FREE things to do in Birmingham' which when I clicked on it started like this:

> 'Birmingham might not sound like a hot destination for tourism, but don't let first impressions fool you. There are a lot of cool things you can do in the city from shopping to nights out. Some of them won't even cost you a penny! From art exhibitions to music concerts and museums, there is a whole array of free things to do in Birmingham. So when are you joining in the fun?
>
> 'Browse all 21 destinations or click on the shortcut names below to jump to a particular attraction.'

There followed a detailed list of free things to do in Birmingham.

I could click on each attraction to find great photographs and a well written piece about each place.

This was on the website of Citybase Apartments which, yes you have guessed it, had apartments available for me to stay at in Birmingham.

The firm knows I'm planning a trip to Birmingham because I'm looking for things to do there. It has sold me on the idea that I should come, and I can book an apartment through the company.

Would I have ended up on its website without that blog? I highly doubt it. In fact, the website is full of useful information for travellers who just so happen to be their target market. There is a blog, as well as sections for news, travel tips, explore destinations and, of course, find apartments.

There are so many advantages to blogging if you have the time to do it properly and effectively. So here are the things you must do if you're going to start writing a blog.

1. **Be consistent.** Most people who blog do the odd one here and there, or for a few weeks and then stop. We're back to the gym analogy. You can't go once every six months and expect results. Sure, it is better than doing nothing – but barely. Similar to networking, the key is consistency. I would recommend writing one blog a week, but the most important thing is to stick at it, even if it is only once a month.

2. **Be an expert**. You have to be talking from a position of authority. No one is going to be interested

in your blog if they think you don't know what you're talking about. It should be related to your business, so you should be an expert. There would be no point me writing a blog about how to do DIY on your investment properties because I am terrible at it and I don't know what I'm talking about. People who do know would soon realise I was an idiot.

3. **Be interesting and informative.** Have a good think about what interests your customers and give them bundles of good content. DON'T SELL. Just give value and then every now and again remind people what you do or how you can help.

4. **Choose a platform.** Whilst blogging can be really productive, other media might be more suited to you and your business such as YouTube videos. In our business we use YouTube videos to great effect. We release nine videos a week on YouTube. These videos are packed with FREE, valuable information for anyone who is serious about investing in property. It took a little while to build up, but at the timing of writing we have over 160,000 YouTube subscribers and we get around a million views per month. One of our videos got 1.5m views.

Almost half our customers come from YouTube, so you can see just how powerful a marketing tool it can be.

The great thing about producing a video is that you get two bites at the cherry as you can then summarise it in a blog.

Chapter 7 - The Sales System

As an entrepreneur, 80% of your time should be focused on sales and marketing.

Now you might be thinking "That's not right, the most important thing is having a great product or service" or "Surely the customer is the most important, my time should be spent on customer service."

While both statements are perfectly valid points, they are unfortunately out of sync with the the world we currently live in; it doesn't matter who has the best product, what matters is whether people know about your products and are they buying them? In an ideal world, of course the company with the best product would win but in the real world, the person with the best sales and marketing wins every time.

Obviously I don't make the rules, but I do want to win in business, so I follow them and you should too.

The first point is that it doesn't matter what business you're in, you just need people to know about you and then want to buy from you.

Sales isn't just important when you're trying to persuade someone from parting with their hard earned cash, but it's also an essential skill when you're selling someone on working for you, partnering with you, buying into your vision etc. You're selling every day, so make sure you're an expert. If there's one sure fire way to help guarantee your business is a success, it's to be good at sales.

Many people think they're just not very good at sales, they're not a natural born salesperson, or that they just don't enjoy it. This is normally because of a bad experience of being rejected or the highly uncomfortable feeling of trying to get someone to agree to something that they clearly don't want to.

I'll be honest, I used to hate sales. I was forced to do it from the age of 16. At the time I didn't even know it was sales but I knew I hated it. As you know, my first job was an entertainer and, of all the different types of entertainment we offered, the thing I found the hardest was Close Up Magic. As a 'close up magician' my job was to go into a restaurant, corporate event or wedding and while people were in between courses or generally socialising, I would have to approach their table and ask if they wanted to see any magic.

Believe it or not, most people just want to chat at a social event and not watch a shy 16 year old in an oversized suit perform card tricks.

The feeling of rejection was real. The jokes were at my expense.

"Why don't you make yourself disappear?" they would scoff, or condescend by saying "I think there are some children over there, why don't you go and see if they're interested!"

I hated approaching people, I felt really awkward and uncomfortable. Even worse, when I was rejected, the surrounding tables would overhear it, making it all the more embarrassing to approach them. However, I was being paid by the client to approach every table so I had no choice but to persevere.

Looking back now, although I didn't realise at the time, this was some of the best sales training I could ever have endured. I learnt all about the assumptive close, body language, positioning myself as an expert, dealing with rejection, believing in my product, the list goes on.

When I hired my first sales person, let's call him David, I was quite surprised at how bad David was at selling. This was someone who had experience in Sales, they'd performed well at previous companies. Why were they unable to perform like me? Why was my conversion rate so much higher than his?

I actually couldn't put my finger on it. Back then, I thought that you were either good at sales or you weren't. You either had the gift of the gab or you didn't.

"What am I doing that he isn't?" I said to my wife.
"Well what do you do?" she asked
I was a little stumped, I wasn't actually sure what I did.
"Errm I don't know, but they want to buy at the end," I replied.
"Well if you don't know, how can you expect him to know!" she said.

She had made a very good point. At that moment, I decided to film myself for an entire day making phone calls and watch to see what I did. After watching the footage back, I realised that subconsciously I had been following a formula the whole time.

So I spent 2 days working with David, teaching him the system, showing him exactly what I did and to my astonishment his sales doubled pretty much overnight.

I suddenly realised that I didn't need to hire experienced sales people, anyone that had good energy and was friendly or likeable would do.

By this time, we were achieving about a 40% conversion rate of our leads, which was unheard of in our industry and now I would like to share this simple but powerful system with you. It's called the W.I.N.N.E.R. Sales System.

W is for Won Over

Before you can sell anything to anyone, you, yourself, need to be won over by the product first. Put simply, to be able to sell effectively, you need to be sold on your product or service.

What I realised, as a 16 year old close up magician, was why everyone was saying no to me. I remember thinking "no wonder everyone's saying no, I don't think I'm very good myself". I didn't believe in my own product, ME.

That was the catalyst for believing in my product - I immediately put all my efforts into practicing and rehearsing my act to make sure I was as good as I could possibly be. I wanted to ensure that they would genuinely be missing out if they said no. And if they did say no, I would make sure that people at nearby tables would say yes. To these tables I would deliver an exceptional service and make so much noise, create such excitement with my perfected tricks that the people who'd originally sent me away, would call me back to entertain them. And that's exactly what happened and that's when I began to love the selling ceremony, and the better I became at it, the more I grew to love it.

The moral of the story is that if you want to be good at sales, you must first make sure that you love your product. Make sure that you would buy your product yourself.

If you already have a business and already have customers, start off by asking all your existing customers why they decided to buy from you. Write it all down. They might say price, customer experience, location, friendly staff, convenience. Whatever they say, start making a list. Then write down all the advantages that you can possibly think of, as to why someone would be better off using your business over a competitor. Be honest because you need to believe it.

Every product that I sell, whether it be a training seminar or an investment opportunity, I only sell if I 100% believe in that product.

What do you do, however, if you have a product or service that you don't believe in?
Easy answer: find something else to sell.

When I started my children's entertainment company I came up with the great idea of selling party bags. It was the perfect upsell.

Mothers would need to organise them anyway, they were on the phone to me, they'd just paid for the entertainment so they were in buying mode anyway, it just made sense.

I found a local company who could arrange the fulfilment, so everything was good to go.
This is how it worked. We would sell the party bags over the phone and charge £2 per bag. We would then send that order over to the party bag company who would send the bags directly to the client's home address and invoice us £1.30 per bag making us a sweet, 70p profit per bag. The average party had 30 children in attendance, meaning an additional £21 direct profit. Easy money.

It sounded perfect, but for some reason we really struggled to sell them. I didn't really mind as it was little effort on our part but it did surprise me. However, I soon came to see things differently.

When it came to my daughter's first birthday party, we arranged for my company to provide the entertainment of course. I totally believed in the product and wouldn't have dreamed of using anyone else. My wife suggested I order some party bags well.
"No, let's make them ourselves" I responded. "Those ones are cheap tat."

That's when I realised why we weren't able to sell them, we didn't believe in them. We thought they were cheap tat, subconsciously we didn't even want the customer to buy them. Even though I knew the first step of selling is "Win Over", I'd ignored my own advice.

So from that day on, when it comes to considering any product, business new venture etc, I make sure I'm 100% won over before I do anything with the idea and you should too.

I is for Investigation

Ok so you're completely sold on your product. You are utterly in love with it, because it is, of course, amazing. Now it's time to actually go out to the market place and sell your offering.

The first thing you should do when you get in contact with a prospect is to investigate. If you do this simple thing, you will be better than 99% of 'professional' sales people because unfortunately 99% of sales people fail to do this.

A couple of years ago, I decided to order a clocking-in machine for our staff. I was being urged to do it by our health and safety officer, in case of a fire. It would also be a great tool for tracking staff hours, overtime etc. So my PA arranged a meeting with a company who offered a top of the range clocking-in machine for companies.

The man arrived in his bright blue three-piece suit, wheeling behind him the oversized machine. So we sat down, he introduced himself and then spent the next 30 minutes telling me about all the machine's amazing features. For example how, if builders were on site, they could log into it with photo recognition, and could even be required to scan their passports for extra security. He told me how schools used it for safeguarding when visitors came onto the premises. He gave me many examples, which, to be honest I wasn't listening to, because I'd switched off. How were these examples relevant to me? We weren't running a school or a building site. Needless to say, I didn't buy the machine.

So what did he do wrong? He was clearly won over by his product. I could see his passion. However, he did what most sales people do, he tried to force his product down my throat without asking whether or not it suited my needs or even asking me what I needed it for.

You've probably experienced something similar maybe at a networking event or over the telephone. In fact most people don't like being sold to as a direct result of someone doing this to them, because it's such a bad sales method. No-one likes to be pressured into buying something that they don't need or want, or where the benefits to them are not made obvious.

So if you don't like being sold to it's probably because of bad sales people who don't know how to investigate your particular needs and make their pitch relevant to you.

Think about it, nearly everyone likes to buy stuff, in fact many of us love to buy. Why? Because we want that item. We like being sold to when it's something we want, we just don't want to be sold to when it's something we don't see any value in.

The salesman in the bright blue suit, who tried to sell me the clocking-in machine didn't ask me what I wanted the machine for. If he had, he would have known that we didn't have any visitors, it was purely for staff. So we didn't need proof of ID! All I wanted was something cheap for staff to sign in and out and so we ended up buying a signing in book for £2.99. If he'd have asked the right questions and presented the right product, I more than likely would have bought the product. Instead, he wasted his time and mine.

The great thing about the WINNER system is that you don't need to pressure anyone. You don't need to sell anything that they don't want. It makes sales way more fun, enjoyable and profitable for you and your prospects.

One of my students at an advanced training programme said to me "It's easy for you, you could sell ice to an Eskimo." I replied "No, I couldn't and even if I could, why on earth would I want to? An Eskimo doesn't need ice. If I sold ice to an Eskimo I'd be doing him a disservice."

Selling is about finding someone's needs and providing the right product for those
needs.

This is far easier if you have leads coming to you. I hate cold calling. I see it as a waste of time, given that most of the people you speak to are the wrong people and most of them aren't interested in what you'll be trying to sell. So I would highly recommend having some way of getting yourself in front of people who are interested. For example, if you've read this book there's a very good chance you'd be interested in attending one of my live business training programmes. So you would be a warm lead.

Let me give you an example of how this works.

I might call you up and say:

"Hi [your name], Russell Leeds here, just a really quick call to see how you're getting on with my book The Entrepreneurs Blueprint?"

Now I'm going to ask you questions to find out where you are on your entrepreneurial journey and more importantly, if I have any products or services that you might want or need. So I'd probably start with something like:

"So why did you decide to order the book"'

Normally the reply would be something vague like:

"I'm interested in entrepreneurship."

So I would have to keep asking questions like "Nice, and why are you interested in entrepreneurship?"

The concept is clear, you just keep asking relevant questions until you feel you have a good understanding of what they want and whether or not you can fulfil their needs.

The type of questions you should be asking are open-ended questions. The dictionary definition of an open-ended question is:

"A question that cannot be answered with a "yes" or "no" response, or with a static response. Open-ended questions are phrased as a statement which requires a response. The response can be compared to information that is already known to the questioner."

So don't ask "Did you like my book?" because they will probably just say "Yes".
Instead, if you ask "Why did you order the book? Or "What were you wanting to get from the book?", you'll find out far more about what they actually want.

The key is just to keep asking questions. They say that the only way to be interesting is to be interested. Show an interest in them, let them speak, find out what they want. The interesting thing is that sometimes they don't even know why or what they want until you ask and it forces them to think about it. So if they are a little vague keep asking "Why?" until you get to the truth and until you know exactly what they want and how you can help.

In essence, you are looking for at least one of two things. Either the customer's "pain", what pain are they in that you can solve? Or their "gain", what can you give them that they would like.

At this point if you can't help, if you are unable to solve their problem or provide them with a gain, just stop the process there and then. Don't waste any more time - yours or theirs. No need to feel rejection. They won't even know that you were selling to them, they'll just think what a nice and interesting person Russell Leeds is to personally call me just for buying his book.

N is for No Brainer

So you've got an amazing product, you've just spent 5 minutes talking to your prospect and you know that it is the perfect product for them and they seriously need it in their life. What now?

You are going to create a no brainer offer for them. You are going to present it in such a way that they would be nuts to say no.

This book is designed to help you scale your business so that you can earn a passive income even if you choose to stop working.

Another fundamental principle of selling is that it is important to rely on a script. If your plan is to grow your business, you will eventually have a sales team. Do you really just want them saying whatever they want? Of course not. You want them to be saying exactly what you want them to say. That way, they can't oversell and promise the earth, or just spout rubbish because they don't really know what to say.

The main reason people dislike scripts is because they're afraid they'll sound robotic. While this is true with many scripts, if you write a good one and learn it off by heart, this will not be the case.

An inspiring speech delivered by a politician, or a gripping movie, will have been scripted and then delivered in such a way that it is not robotic. Your job is to do the same with your sales script.

It is one of the most important parts of your business because without making sales you have no business – certainly not a business that will make any money.

So let me take you through some tips on crafting a good script. First of all, the greeting. You do not want to sound like a typical salesman, especially if you're the one making the call.

Each script should be made up of two parts:

1.The Introduction

How many times have you answered the phone and immediately identified that it's just a sales call and switch off immediately? It might sound something like this:

> Salesman: "Hello my name is David calling from Premier Insurance Limited. Could I speak to Russell Leeds, please?"
>
> You know it's a sales call straight away and normally you can hear other people in the background. It sounds like a call centre.

You want to avoid this.

I start the conversation with something friendly and simple such as:

"Hi, is that Zoe?"

> It makes me sound like I know her slightly and just using her first name is far more personable.

I then introduce myself just by giving my name and the company name:
"My name's Russell Leeds calling from Property Investors with Samuel Leeds."

I do not recommend cold calling. It annoys people, as well as being time-consuming, and it is very difficult to get results. I only call people when they have taken an action first, such as ordered a book or filled in an enquiry form on our website. This makes calling people far easier as you are only ringing individuals who are genuinely interested in your product or service.

The next step is to give the reason I'm calling Zoe, as follows:

> "The reason I'm calling today is I noticed you've recently ordered a copy of Samuel's book "*Buy Low Rent High"* and I'm just checking that you've received it."

Notice that at this point there is no selling, this is now the time for the investigation.
I recommend having a few set questions to start your investigation, and you should write these down as part of your script.

2. Selling

This is where you will put together your no brainer offer.

It's now time to highlight the benefits of what you have to offer. Remember you're helping this person and you're an expert at what you do, so don't be modest and hold back. If your product is awesome and is going to fulfil their needs, tell them it is and tell them why. That is why you should have a script. It gives you time to relay all the benefits and reasons they should use you. And that's when you give them the price.

Remember the list that you made at the beginning of this chapter? When you were winning yourself over? You are now going to write some sales copy for each of those points and you're going to put them in your script.

When you're writing your sales copy, the most important thing you can do is focus on the benefits not the features.

Let me give you an example:

> I wanted to buy a new laptop recently so I headed down to my local PC World to have a browse. I wanted to see the laptop physically before buying it. The store assistant approached me and asked:

"Can I help you?"

"I'm looking for a new laptop" I replied.

> "We've got this one on sale," he eagerly told me. "It's a Windows 10, it has a AMD a Ryzen 3 3200U processor, it's got 4 GB of RAM and 256 GB of storage."
>
> Now for computer dummies, like me, he might as well have been speaking a foreign language. He was just giving me the features. He wasn't giving me the benefits.

What we need to remind ourselves is that we know far more about our product and the industry than our clients do. We might understand all the features and exactly what they mean, but there's a very good chance that most of our clients don't know what these mean.

The PC World store assistant knew exactly what it meant but I didn't. So you need to know the features but then tell the client how that feature will benefit them.

So instead, he should have asked this:

> "So what are you planning to use the computer for?"
>
> I might have replied "Well mainly for watching movies on Netflix while I'm travelling, for browsing the internet and editing photos."
>
> From those answers, he could have told me the features and related the benefits to me. He could have said:

> "Ah we have this one on sale which has a AMD Ryzen 3 3200U processor which means that your Netflix movies will stream almost instantly and 256GB of storage so you can store and edit over 10,000 photos."

Before any computer experts call me out on this example, I am making it up, but hopefully you understand the point. The salesman is giving me the features and explaining why they'll benefit me.

Let me give you another example. Here is some sales copy that I wrote for a three-day programme that we run, teaching people how to make money from property starting with no money, using a strategy called 'Rent to Rent'.

Rent 2 Rent Revolution

> *"How to make £1,000s or even £10,000s a month without even owning any property!"*
>
> Nelson Rockefeller famously said,
>
> > *"The secret to success is to own nothing, but control everything."*
>
> Multi million-pound companies understand this very well. For example, Uber doesn't own the cars that transport you, Airbnb don't own the accommodation you book through them and Amazon don't own the majority of the stock they distribute around the world.

> You too can use the power of leverage once you've attended this life changing programme.

You'll learn:

- How to generate 'Super Rent' so you can maximise profits from any property;
- How to find the right properties online - you'll actually find potential deals there and then;
- The magic words you'll need to say to seal the deal, so that you can start making money almost immediately; and
- How to systemise your business to ensure a hands-off approach to property management and the creation of passive income.

Now notice the use of a "feature" versus a "benefit". There are a couple of examples.

> "How to generate Super Rent" - this is the feature and people might not know what it means, so I explain what's in it for them as a benefit by saying "so that you can maximise the profits from any property."

And

> "How to systemise" this is the feature, and the benefit is "to ensure a hands off approach to

> property management and to create passive income."

Steve Jobs was the master of this. When he sold the iPod to the world back in 2001, he used the slogan "1000 songs in your pocket". The slogan wasn't "the iPod has a 5GB hard drive and FireWire technology." He went straight to the benefit.

So make a list of all the features of your product and why they're a massive benefit to your potential customer.

The other thing to be sure to include is social proof. This can be testimonials, awards, if you've featured in the press, had celebrity or well-known companies as clients and so on.

It's one thing you saying how great your company is, but it takes it to another level when you can share third party data and it's a very powerful sales tool.

Now to package your no brainer, you're going to start with the pain or the gain they told you about during the investigation stage. So for example:

> "Now as you've just said you're desperate to leave your job and be your own boss but just don't know where to start. And you know that if you just carry on the way you are, it'll never get better..."
>
> So you're highlighting the problem they've just told you about. Once you've done this, you'll then tell them about a few of the features and benefits from

your list, but be sure to choose those that are most relevant to them.

Less is more in many cases, you don't want to just go on and on. People don't have the time or the patience to listen to you rambling on about irrelevancies. Just pick 2 or 3 of the most relevant features and tell them why they need your product in their life, and explain why it will help them solve their problems.

N is for Negotiation

This is the part that people tend to omit. They finish the sales part and then just stop, hoping that the prospect will say:

> "Yes, I'm in. Sign me up."

Sorry to break it to you (although I'm sure you already know), but that rarely happens.

It's now time to negotiate and this starts with 'the close'. A lot of people are scared of closing because this is where they fear rejection, but this is the time to ask for the sale.

There is a popular sales strategy - "Always Be Closing" - the ABC of sales. However this is simply nonsense. You should not be closing until your prospect is ready to be closed. I never close unless I'm confident that they want what I'm selling. If you close too early you risk just annoying them.

There are tons and tons of great closes.

One of my favourites is the assumptive close. This is where you've just finished your sale and then you ask a question. This question is assuming that they are ready to buy, so you would say something like "How would you like to pay?"

I'll never forget when someone replied "I don't want to pay." Ouch, did I feel rejected and a little embarrassed? You bet. Why did she say that? Because I closed too early. I closed before she was ready.

So before you close, you need to know 2 things:

1. Do they want and/or need your product?
2. Do they trust you to provide what you say you will provide?

You should have a good feeling for this during the Investigation and No Brainer part of the process. If you think they're ready, then that is the time to close.

Another version of the assumptive close that I really like is the '3 Yes Assumptive Close.'

You ask three questions that you know they'll say yes to and then you ask for the sale. It has got them in the habit of saying 'yes' and admitting out loud that it is something they want. An example might be:

> "So, let me get this straight, you want to get into property investing?" (Yes)
> "You're wanting to start earning a passive income?" (Yes)
> "And you think the training we provide would be of benefit to you?" (Yes)
> "Well what are we waiting for? Shall we get you signed up?" (Yes!)

Another favourite of mine is the 'Alternative Close' this is where you offer 2 alternatives both of which involve them buying your product. So you might say:

> "Would you like to attend the course this Wednesday or next Wednesday?"
>
> Effectively, you're offering them this Wednesday which is a sale or next Wednesday which is also a sale.

Be sure to pick a few closes that you feel comfortable with and make sure they work for your product.

So by this stage, you've got an awesome product that you love, you've investigated your prospect and you know they need your product. You then package together a no brainer offer that will make it virtually impossible for them to say no to, right? Wrong. They will almost always say 'no' at this point. Well not normally an outright no, they'll come up with an excuse as to why they can't commit at that precise moment.

Why do people do that? It's because most people hate making a decision, they like to think about things first. They put off making a decision because it's easier than actually making a decision.

Once you have closed there are two options:

1 - They buy.
2 - They say no or come up with objections.

Most of the time, when someone gives an objection, whatever they say is not always true. It is often just an excuse not to buy. Your job as a salesperson is to try to get to the bottom of the real reason for objecting to the sale. Let me give you an example from Grant Cardone's book.

They might say to you:
"I need to speak to my wife."

> Now I want to find out whether this is a true objection or if they're just looking for an excuse not to buy and the real objection is something else.

So I would reply with:

> "I totally understand, no problem, can I ask you a question what will you do if your wife says no?"

They have three possible responses:

1. "My wife won't say no."
2. "If she says no, I'll do it anyway."
3. "If she says no, I won't buy."

If they go for option 1 or 2, it sounds to me like they are ready to buy.

If they reply with option 3, I would ask:

"And why do you think she would say no?"

> When they tell you the reason, this is not really coming from the wife. It is coming from him.
>
> If he says: "she'll think it's too expensive", ask yourself who really thinks it's too expensive? Is it the

> wife (who doesn't even know the price) or is it really him?

So now you know the real reason why the person may not be ready to buy. They think it's too expensive. Well that's not strictly true, most people won't think it's too expensive. What they really think is that it's too expensive for what you are selling.

They think that the price you are asking is higher than the value of the product. Something to bear in mind is that the decision whether to buy or not is always about value and never about price.

Here's an example:

> If I said give me £10,000 for my iPhone that's worth £1,000, you'd say "No that's too expensive" or "I can't afford it", but if I said give me £10,000 for a Ferrari that is worth £200,000, you'd suddenly be able to find £10,000. You'd beg, borrow and steal to get that £10,000 to get the bargain of the century. Why? Because the value of the product has changed, not the price.

It's never the price, it's always the value.

So if someone thinks your product is too expensive it means you haven't done a good enough job of selling.

I recommend making a note of every objection you encounter and writing it down. Then think about a good way of answering that objection and include it in your script. Believe it or not, there are normally only about 10 different objections that people will come up with for any given product. So just make sure you know what objections to expect and be ready with an answer to each of these so you can get to the truth.

There are two things to remember when considering your responses:

1. Always agree with your prospect or at the very least understand and acknowledge what they're saying.

   So let's say I'm selling the 'Winner Sales Intensive' two-day programme and after I close, someone says:
   "Sounds good but I need to think about it."

   I would respond:
   "Of course, I totally understand, how long would you like to think about it? Couple of days? Couple of weeks?"

   So now I've agreed with what they've said and I've demonstrated that I understand where they're coming from. This takes away any argument.

   Most sales people would say something like "What is there to think about?"

The problem with that approach is that it's aggressive. You should always start the closing process with agreement not aggression.

I know a sales person who when told by a prospect "I need to check with my wife" , asked him "Do you run every little decision past your wife?" What a way to turn off the customer and lose the sale! Always start by agreeing or at least understanding.

2. Offer an alternative idea.

Once you've agreed with your prospect, you can offer an alternative point of view. This often works best in the form of questions.

So if we go back to our "sounds good but I need to think about it" example, I would then say:
"Can I be totally honest with you? There are only 3 things to think about, do you mind if I share them with you?" They usually say yes and I ask them:

1. Are you serious about becoming better at sales? (Yes)
2. If you absolutely had to, could you afford it? (Yes)
3. Do you think you'd find the programme valuable? (Yes)

Well if you answer yes to all those 3 questions, there's nothing left for you to think about - you're going to get a load of value, you want to do it, so come on let's do this, how would you like to pay? In full or in instalments?"

So I've agreed with them and now offered them an alternative point of view.

It makes your life so much easier if you properly prepare for when people throw excuses at you and remember they are just excuses. They are excuses made to save them from making a decision. When you really believe in your product and you know that it offers real value, just remember that it only gives value to people when they buy. If they don't actually buy, all you've done is waste their time. If they need or want your product, make sure that you hang in there.

Take your time to craft your responses. Believe me, if you do this, it will put you in the top 1% of all sales people.

R is for Repeat

This is the final step in the WINNER sales system and probably the most important.

So you've just eliminated the excuse to get to the real reason why they're not ready to buy and now you need to repeat the system.

If you remember when we wrote down all the selling points during the 'No Brainer' section, I said only use a couple of them and leave some out.

Think of those selling points as ammo in your gun. You don't want to unload all your ammo in one go or there will be nothing left. If they don't buy at the first attempt, you'll have nothing left to say without just repeating yourself. However, if you keep some back, once you've eliminated their excuses, you can now repeat the process but this time with fresh features and benefits to use.

You should move back into the 'No Brainer Section' then 'Negotiate' then 'Eliminate Excuses' and if necessary 'Repeat' again.

This is why it's so important to have lots of selling points in your script but not to use them all at once. You should use the most relevant ones first, but if you need to resell, leave things available to say without just repeating yourself.

To sum up, you sell and then you close. If they don't buy, you move onto the second sales script and then close. If they don't buy again, move onto the third sales script and then close. Obviously, only do this if they are genuinely interested. Don't just keep hammering away if they're not interested and are giving you an outright 'no.' This is designed for people who are on the fence and you are trying to gently nudge them over.

After Sales

The after sales process is almost just as important as the sales process itself. If you're going to take one piece of advice from this chapter, it would be this: TRACK EVERYTHING.

I use a sales spreadsheet to track all my enquiries. This has been set up on Google Sheets and is stored in the Cloud. The reason I use a Google Sheets Spreadsheet and not a Microsoft Excel Spreadsheet is because having it stored in the Cloud is really useful.

The main advantage is that all your staff or even just your business partner if you prefer, can access your sales spreadsheet at the same time. Therefore, you see when someone else makes a change in real time. You're also not risking losing loads of work as it automatically saves and backs up as you go.

Your sales spreadsheet is going to be the cornerstone of all your sales and marketing activity.

So let's take a look at what your sales spreadsheet should look like. Along the top row, each in their own column, I have the following:

> Staff Name, Date of Enquiry, Phone, Email, Name, Product Required, Additional Information, Where Are They Based, Date Required, Quote, Next Action, Have They Bought? If Not, Why Not? Time They Booked, How Did They Find Us?

Now I'm going to explain why I have each one of these, although you will most likely have to edit this to fit your business.

Staff Name – The name of the member of staff dealing with the enquiry. This is useful to know who the customer has spoken to.

Date of Enquiry – Especially useful for looking back to see how many enquiries you received on a given day and comparing year on year.

Phone – I have found that potential customers who have provided us with a phone number are far more likely to buy. This is because selling over the phone is much more effective than selling by email.

Email – Take down the prospect's email address and email them regularly to stay in touch. We'll explore this further when we look at the Next Action box.

Name – Write down the person's name and make sure you regularly use it when having a conversation with them.

Dale Carnegie, author of the brilliant book, "*How to Win Friends and Influence People*", says this:

> "*Remember that a person's name is to that person the sweetest and most important sound in any language. Using a person's name is crucial, especially when meeting those we don't see very*

> *often. Respect and acceptance stem from simple acts such as remembering a person's name and using it whenever appropriate."*

Product required – The product or service that they're interested in.

Additional Information – Any additional information that would be useful to you. This may be regarding the product itself, for example, they only want a yellow one. I primarily use this box to write down information about the client. I'll give you an example:

> I called a lady and she advised me she couldn't talk right now as she was taking her little girl, Amy, to hospital and could I call back in a few days. She sounded stressed, so I quickly ended the call and made a note in the Additional Information box.
>
> A few days later, when I called back, I started off by asking how Amy was and what had happened. She, of course, appreciated that I had not only remembered the situation but also remembered Amy's name. She went on to buy and I got the sale.

At that time, I was calling about 50 people every day. Would I have remembered if I had not written it down? Highly unlikely. Instead of appearing to be thoughtful and caring, I would have come across as rude and uncaring. Would I have got the sale? Probably not.

Make sure you use this box to take an interest in your customers.

Where Are They Based – This may or may not be relevant to your business.

Date Required? – Again, this is only really relevant for a service-based business.

Quote – If you quote different amounts depending on where someone is based or the size of the job, make sure you know how much you have quoted them to avoid sounding incompetent.

Next Action – This box is certainly the most important one when it comes to sales. If anyone makes an enquiry and leaves a phone number, make sure you call them. If they don't answer the phone, I send them a text message explaining who I am and why I'm calling them.

I will then attempt to call them three times that day at different times – normally morning, afternoon and evening.

I'll try this again for the next few days. However, if someone has not answered after 12 calls I give up, as either they are deliberately ignoring me, I have a wrong number or for some reason they are clearly unable to answer their phone.

This is all marked in the next action box. Let's say I attempt to call someone on June 11th in the morning. I would write NA x 1 - 11/6 m.

NA – stands for Not Answered
x 1 – how many times I have attempted to call
11/6 – the date
M – indicates that it is in the morning

If they didn't answer again in the afternoon, I would change it to NA x 2 -11/6 ma. And so on.

Once you've managed to get hold of your prospect and have delivered your well-crafted sales pitch, sometimes they're not in a situation where they're ready to buy yet. The Rule of Seven is an old saying in marketing. It basically means that someone would have to hear from you seven times before they are in a situation where they are ready to buy. Obviously, it is not always seven times, but don't give up on someone just because they don't buy the first time you speak to them.

Normally they'll say something like: "I just need to compare a few more quotes", "I need to talk to my partner" or "let me have a couple of days to think about it."

Most people say: "Yes sure, no problem" and guess what? Most of the time you will never hear from them again.

Make sure that when you put the phone down, you're in control of the conversation. For example:

> If they say: "I need to talk to my partner" and after investigation, as above, this is genuine, I would say:

"No problem, when do you think you'd be able to talk to them?"

"Well he's working late tonight, so tomorrow (Tuesday)," they reply.

"No problem, well if I don't hear from you before, shall I give you a call back on Wednesday at say 11am?" I ask.

Now 95 percent of the time they will agree to this. So, I would write on my sales spreadsheet – interested call back Wednesday 12/6 11:00am to close the deal.

Always call people back when you say you are going to. It certainly builds up the trust element, proving that you deliver on what you say you are going to do.

If they're still not ready to buy, repeat this and stay in control of the conversation.

If at any point through this process someone asks not to be called back and says something like: "If I decide I want to buy, I'll call you", it is their way of politely telling you they are not interested.

So just write a big NO in the Next Action Box and do not call them again.

Even though I don't waste time calling again, I will continue to stay in touch with them through email. When someone makes an initial enquiry, I will email them every day for the first week and then continue to email after that, albeit more infrequently.

It doesn't have to just be sales letters; you should be sending useful information regarding the product or service that they're considering purchasing. This is a great way of staying in the forefront of your prospect's mind while they're making a buying decision.

This is, of course, all automated, set up in the background to be working automatically without you having to actually do anything. The beauty of automated email is that it does not take rejection personally. It carries on regardless and it doesn't quit because someone shows a lack of interest.

Quite regularly someone will call to say they wish to make a booking and, when I find their name on the sales spreadsheet, they have a big NO in the Next Action box. I smile to myself that our software system has gained us another client quietly in the background.

If you haven't already got an automated email system set up, you're missing a trick. Do it now! We currently use Infusionsoft, but there are lots of other cheaper software options and even some that are free. Mailchimp, for example, is free, depending on the amount of email addresses in your list.

Have They Bought? – If a person has not bought, I write No in this box. If they have bought, I write the information contained in the 'How did they find us' box, for example Facebook.

I do this so that I can use the COUNTIF formula to search that column and find out how many bookings have come from Facebook, internet search, a recommendation or another way, without having to manually add them all up myself. This probably saves me 30-45 minutes a month and is another good example of systemising.

If Not, Why Not? – You will not get an answer from everybody, but it is really useful asking people why they have decided to go with someone else and not buy from you. Once you know the reason, write it down in this box.

Keep an eye on this and if you notice the same reasons coming up again and again, maybe it is time to adapt so that it stops happening.

When we first started using the sales board for *Non Stop Kids Entertainment*, I noticed that quite a lot of people were saying what we provided was too expensive.

Our main product was a two-hour complete party package priced at £199.

So we added an extra package which we did not advertise on the website but could offer if someone said the party was too expensive.

We introduced a 90-minute package for £169. We booked in at least five of these packages per month. These were all extra bookings that we would not have obtained had we not used the sales spreadsheet.

Time They Bought? – Every time you make a sale note the time in this box. If the time was 10:32, I just input 10 to show the hour that it was made. This is a new column that I have added recently. The idea of this column is that we can track the busiest times in the office. What times are we most likely to be making sales? Again, you can use the COUNTIF formula to calculate this for you.

If we have to arrange staff meetings, training or even when staff have breaks, it's useful to know when the quietest times are and when sales will be affected the least.

How Did They Find Us? – From what marketing activity did the person find your company and make that enquiry? This could be Facebook, a recommendation, or a previous client.

It is really important that every time somebody makes an enquiry, they get put on this spreadsheet. We have an enquiry form on our website. When a prospect fills in the form, Infusionsoft automatically adds all their details to the spreadsheet for us. However, if somebody calls us, we have to manually add the information.

Once it gets to the end of the month, you have a wealth of really useful data to have a look at. You will have information such as:

- How many enquiries you've had
- A breakdown of where all those enquiries have come from
- How many sales you've had
- A breakdown of where all those sales have come from
- What your conversion rate is i.e. how many enquiries you need to make a sale
- You can also compare conversion rates depending where the enquiry has come from
- The peak times for sales in the office
- What the average sale price is
- Compare average sales price depending on where the enquiry has come from

This means you can look at your marketing spend. For example:

> Say I spent £500 on Facebook ads and it generated 50 enquiries at a cost of £10 per enquiry.
>
> We then made 20 sales from those 50 enquiries at a conversion rate of 40 percent, costing us £25 per sale.
>
> The average sale price was £200 which means you have an eight-times return on investment.

Now do this for all of your marketing activities so you can see which strategies are working the best. Once you know this, it becomes really clear where you should invest your marketing budget.

You can see what is working and what is not working. This information is vital in growing your business.

Chapter 8 - Be The Best You Can Be

The Entrepreneur's Blueprint is a fantastic model that many of my students have followed to create highly successful businesses. However there is one potential problem with this model that will stop it from working for you and that potential problem is in fact YOU.

A friend of mine recently joined a new gym, she got given a fantastic diet and exercise plan that would make her super fit and healthy. However after 2 weeks she stopped going, the diet and exercise plan were out of the window. She was super excited and motivated but as soon as that excitement waned, she went back to her normal thinking and she just stopped.

Why do we do that? Look at how many people join the gym or make new year's resolutions in January only to have given up before the end of the month.

It all sounds very simple, it's very easy to be slim or successful, but most of us just don't have the discipline to keep it up.

It all starts in our head. Our thoughts lead to our feelings. Our feelings lead to our actions. Our actions lead to results. So your life, your success, your outcome is all controlled by your thoughts.

We think about 80,000 thoughts a day and according to scientist Dawson Church, about 95% of those thoughts are repetitive and about 80% of those thoughts are negative.

So in other words, we keep thinking the same negative thoughts everyday so of course we are going to keep getting the exact same results. The problem is that most of these thoughts are in our subconscious which means we're not even fully aware of them.

So how on earth do you control 80,000 thoughts that are going on in your subconscious mind?

The answer is you control your environment. We are massively influenced by our environment - that could be our friends, family, workplace, books we read, tv shows we watch, social media, the news, the list goes on.

Jim Rohn famously stated "You are an average of the five people you spend most of your time with." He knew the massive influence other people have on our lives and our thinking.

Just look at how you talk, dress and what you believe. It's a direct result of the people around you and in your society. If you had been born in a different country or 100 years ago, just imagine how different you would be.

I'd like to share with you some tips to help shape your environment to one of positivity and success.

1. Believe in Yourself

Believe in yourself. It makes me sad the amount of talented people who underestimate themselves and as a result take no action.

You can do ANYTHING you want to. I never want to hear any of my students say: "I'm not very good at sales" or "I'll never understand how to do marketing."

Sure, you'll have certain strengths and weaknesses, and you want to play to your strengths. However, if there is anything you really want to do, and you're prepared to put in the effort and time into practising or achieving, you will be able to become a master at whatever you want to do.

I can highly recommend a very interesting book called "*Bounce - The Myth Of Talent And The Power Of Practice*". It's written by a British journalist, author and broadcaster named Matthew Syed, who used to be an international table tennis star and for years was the British number one.

The basic premise of the book, and Matthew has clearly done his research, is that with purposeful practice, we can become experts at anything we set our minds to. If you want it badly enough to put in the practice, you will become world class at it.

In our society we often believe that when someone is good at something, it's in their DNA, but the truth is that unless it is something like basketball, where height is a massive advantage, you could learn to be as good as anyone.

He looks in detail at great sportsmen and women such as Serena and Venus Williams who have dominated tennis for so many years. He highlights the fact that their father chose this path for them and used to make them practise every single day for hours on end. The conclusion is that is why they are so good.

It's called the 10,000-hour rule. If you put in 10,000 hours of purposeful practice, no matter who you are, you will become world class at almost anything. Obviously just to become very good requires far less time.

Once you realise this, and truly believe this, it is liberating as it puts you back in control of your own destiny. Do not make excuses or blame people. Understand that you make your own luck and if you want to be an expert at running a business you absolutely can be –
no matter what your background, gender, race, experience or lack of education.

2. Keep Learning

Property is the second-best investment you can make. The best is in yourself. So never stop educating and investing in yourself. And if you want to invest in property, go to our www.property-investors.co.uk website. There is a ton of FREE stuff on there to get you started.

I absolutely love to keep learning, and one of my daily routines is to read. I read a mixture of business and personal development books. I personally use an app on my phone called Audible. It is owned and run by Amazon and is awesome.

I like to save time wherever possible, so listening to books while I'm driving, walking or even at the gym is ideal. With Audible you can download a new book every month and save it in your library for a small monthly fee. Some audio books are even free. You'd be crazy not to tap into this rich mine of information, if you don't already.

I mentioned earlier that "you are an average of the five people you spend most of your time with." We are so fortunate that we live in a social world where we don't have to physically spend time with people to reap the benefits. If I listen to Jim Rohn's books for 1 hour per day suddenly Jim Rohn is one of the 5 people that I'm influenced by.

This is a fantastic way to change your environment because you have access to all these amazing successful people at the click of a button. Commit to listening everyday, even if it's only 20 minutes. I've found that "reading" one book a month is about perfect for me, as I often listen to the same one up to three times if I like it.

I also like to attend a live training programme or event 4 or 5 times a year. As well as learning highly useful information, there's nothing quite like the energy and connections you make with like-minded people when you attend a live training programme. I've made some great friends and even found business partners and staff from live training events.

3. Be grateful

Be grateful for all the good things in your life. A daily practice of mine is to think of and write down everything I'm grateful for. It could be your wife, children, house, car, best friend, holidays, computer, food, water, clients, money – whatever it is, make a note of it. Even if it is small, remember there are people in this world who do not have those blessings.

When you do this, you'll automatically start to feel more positive and upbeat, and when things do go wrong, you'll be better placed to take full responsibility and to make yourself accountable.

Avoid blaming your staff, because ultimately, you hired them. As soon as you start to take responsibility, you have the power to fix the problem so that it won't happen again.

As well as being grateful, stop moaning about anything. Put a ban on moaning and negativity. Some people do not realise just how much they moan. It's almost as though they actively enjoy moaning and spreading unhappiness, almost like filling a void in their lives or trying to give themselves meaning. But there are so many more productive ways to give yourself meaning!

Remember that constantly being negative, blaming others and moaning will hamper your success; it will block growth and visionary thinking.

Whatever you focus your attention on, you will attract more of that in your life. If you focus on the positives of your team and successful outcomes, you will attract more of those. If you focus on the negatives and the problems, you will attract more problems. So look for the good and regularly praise others.

4. Treat people as you want to be treated

I am a big believer in this philosophy. If you want to be successful and respected, I think that you should be too. Whether you're a believer in God, Mother Universe or other powers such as Karma, it's beneficial to you to treat all people with respect and compassion. You want to be successful, but you certainly don't want to trample over people to get there. You want to become successful by bringing value to people and in turn they will pay you for it.

If you treat your staff well, in the way you would like to be treated, they are far more likely to be loyal to you, happy in their work and buy into what you are trying to achieve, as well as into your vision. They will work harder and be more committed to the company and the cause. They are also more likely to recommend your business to friends and family.

The same goes for your customers. Treat your customers well and they will be loyal for life, but you should also treat your haters with respect. It's so easy to get angry when someone leaves you an unfair review, especially if they leave it in a public place like social media. A natural reaction would be to jump down their throats and attack them in a way that exposes their flawed logic. However, it is far more productive, to be the bigger person and to communicate with respect. It will take the wind out of their sails and sometimes even win them around. I've had people leave a bad review when maybe we haven't been perfect. I've quickly apologised and suggested how we can make it right and sometimes these people turn into your biggest fans.

5. Take Action

Many people fancy the idea of setting up their own business but never do because they're afraid. You don't need to have all the answers, you don't need to know everything. If you know what you want to do, just believe in yourself and do it.

Henry Ford famously said,

> *"Whether you think you can, or you think you can't - you're right."*

I would encourage you to believe in yourself, if there is something you want to do, just do it. If you follow the relatively simple steps outlined in this book, you can run the business of your dreams and just you believing that is enough to actually make it come true.

Something I have to drum home to many of my students is to stop worrying about the XYZ before you have done the ABC. So many people don't take action because they're worried about potential problems in the future. Don't be that person.

When writing this book, the ABC was to just start writing it. I could be asking myself questions like how will I find a publisher, what do I do if no one reads it or even what should the title be? All that's going to do is stop me from taking action now. Those will be problems I need to worry about in the future, those are what I call the XYZ questions.

A famous biblical quote comes to mind

> *"Therefore do not worry about tomorrow, for tomorrow will worry about itself. Each day has enough trouble of its own."*

Don't let anything stop you from following your dreams and living the life that you want to live.

Please do keep in touch:

My personal website is www.russell-leeds.com

Facebook: just search Russell Leeds

Instagram: my username is russellleeds

Check out my website for free content and training events to help aid your journey of success.

Last but not least, thank you for taking the time to read my book.

Printed in Great Britain
by Amazon

39108754R00090